MORE STUDIO TIPS

for artists and graphic designers

BILL GRAY

PRENTICE HALL PRESS • NEW YORK

Books by Bill Gray

STUDIO TIPS FOR ARTISTS AND GRAPHIC DESIGNERS (1976)
MORE STUDIO TIPS FOR ARTISTS AND GRAPHIC DESIGNERS (1978)
LETTERING TIPS FOR ARTISTS, GRAPHIC DESIGNERS, AND CALLIGRAPHERS (1980)
TIPS ON TYPE (1983)

To Karen and Alex, with love.

Copyright © 1978 by Prentice Hall Press
A Division of Simon & Schuster, Inc.
All rights reserved, including the right of reproduction
in whole or in part in any form.

Published in 1986 by Prentice Hall Press
A Division of Simon & Schuster, Inc.
Gulf + Western Building
One Gulf + Western Plaza
New York, NY 10023

Originally published by Van Nostrand Reinhold Company Inc.

PRENTICE HALL PRESS is a trademark of Simon & Schuster, Inc.

Library of Congress Cataloging-in-Publication Data
Gray, Bill
   More studio tips for artists and graphic designers.
Includes index
1. Drawing—Technique.   2. Graphic arts—Technique
3. Artist's materials.   I. Title—
NC735.G68   702.'8   77-10676
ISBN 0-671-60803-7

Manufactured in the United States of America

10   9   8   7   6   5   4   3   2

Contents

Foreword

This book is a continuation of the first book "Studio Tips," and the purpose of writing it is the same — the hints and tips are presented to make the information immediately available to all graphic artists, whether they are students or practicing professionals, to help solve graphic art problems, and perhaps save time and money as well.

With a few exceptions, all the art and lettering were drawn in the same size as they appear here. It was a labor of love and the writer enjoyed every minute of working on it.

Grateful acknowledgment is given herewith to Susie Short and Bill Fischer for their generous help, and to Wendy Lochner for arranging and organizing the work and editing the copy. Special thanks go to Walter Dew of ATA for permission to reprint the material on page 41.

Business

Tips on getting a job

The following items are listed in no particular order, but all are sig-nicant in getting a job, whether it's your first or fiftieth.

1. Make sure that you have an appointment and don't be late. Don't ever come to an art office cold without being expected.

2. Have a clean portfolio – it doesn't have to be an expensive one. You will not get a job on the leather but what's inside.

3. Put into your portfolio your best work only, even though it may be only a few pieces.

4. If you are showing watercolors or prints, mat them.

5. Keep pieces relatively the same size. If this is not possible, mat the small-er pieces or put two or more small ones on one mat.

6. Neatness and cleanliness count for your art as well as for yourself.

7. If you have worked before, have an extra resumé to leave. Your resumé should show address, schools, prizes, interests, photo of yourself, etc.

8. If you have 3-dimensional material, have photos of it to show.

9. Be pleasant. No-one wants to work with a sourpuss. Don't oversell your-self. Talk little – not excessively or loudly.

10. Never borrow someone else's art to show as your own.

11. Don't say that copied art is original. "They" know.

12. Don't repeat too much of the same thing. Show variety if possible. Portfolios get to be heavy with an excess of similar pieces.

13. If you don't get a job leave in a pleasant way, thanking "them" for their time. They may need you in a few months.

How to run a small art service in your own home

A young artist with talent and enthusiasm can start a small art service at home. If equipment such as a copier machine, multigraph machine, typewriter, and photostat machine is available, it will make your work much easier. Samples of your art that relate to what prospective clients can use and samples of work that you have done for others should be included in a portfolio to show new customers. An example of what you can do is shown below.

You can make your own silkscreens for display art in color after printing all the copies on copier.

YOUR ART

The layout above will never win an art director's award. It is shown as a simple example of what a resourceful artist can do. Stencils for typewritten

Transfer lettering sheets, all styles, can be composed and photostated larger or smaller to fit your layout.

matter can be positioned and "cut" on a typewriter. Other elements can be silkscreened or photostated after manipulation and positioned on the master paste-up. Final copies can be printed in quantity on the copier before silkscreening.

Get an education from reading art dealers' catalogs

Reading good art dealers' catalogs is a splendid way to obtain not only all kinds of information about the tools of the craft but also a complete orientation as to what supplies are available. You may be surprised to find that that thing you saw in a studio is for making ellipses, for example. Many good catalogs are full of informative material such as where the hair for the best artists' brushes comes from.

And they are free!!
(IN MOST PLACES)

The four major processes of printing

The four processes of printing are shown below. The difference in the plates is the major difference in the process, although there are many others that are important – the construction of the machines, the kinds of paper and ink best for each, etc.

LETTERPRESS
(RELIEF PROCESS)

INK — NONPRINTING PARTS

METAL PLATE

Letterpress is the oldest printing method. The raised parts of the plate are inked and print the image when impressed onto the paper. Most letterpress plates are made from metal. All metal type (foundry and machine) is a form of letterpress.

LITHOGRAPHY
(PLANIGRAPHIC PROCESS)

INK — NONPRINTING PARTS

THIN METAL PLATE

Lithography (offset in commercial printing) prints images by dampening the surface of the plate (the nonprinting parts) with moisture and preparing the image area to receive the greasy ink. Printing is possible because grease rejects water.

GRAVURE
(INTAGLIO PROCESS)

INK — NONPRINTING PARTS

METAL PLATE

Gravure (usually rotogravure, because the plate is a large circular cylinder) is the opposite of letterpress. The plate is inked and the nonprinting raised parts of the plate are wiped clean by a "doctor blade."

SILKSCREEN
(STENCIL PROCESS)

INK — SILK — INK (PAINT)

BLOCKOUT STENCIL

Silkscreen is the only method in which, with the use of a rubber squeegee, the paint, or ink, is squeezed through the plate. The blockout is the stencil adhered to the silk. It is hand-cut or composed photographically.

Other processes or methods of printing

There are other printing processes, but they are used mostly for small runs. The one exception is Flexography, which is extremely fast.

Flexography is a letterpress method in which fast-drying inks are used on speed presses. The process is designed for printing on cellophane (bags, covers, etc.). It is a major process in terms of volume of work. It prints from rubber plates.

Colotype is a gelatin process in which the plate "absorbs" the image so that it can be inked and impressed onto paper. Tone areas in the art are not screened, as in other processes, and the printed images are continuous in tone. This technique is used almost exclusively for picture postcards. It is one of the few processes that prints continuous-tone impressions.

Mimeograph is an office machine that prints by a stencil method similar to silk screen. Images can be drawn on the stencil.

Direct Lithography images are drawn in reverse on a large stone with a greasy solution. The nonprinting parts are moistened with water. The resulting lithographs (Daumier, Munch, etc.) tend to be in the fine-arts area and are seldom used in commercial printing, except to furnish a print for further reproduction by one of the major processes. Lithographs have a grainy look.

Etchings and Woodcuts are also in the fine-arts area. Etching (intaglio) and woodcut (relief) prints, however, can be used for reproduction by other commercial processes.

Photographs and Photostats are photographic processes and are related to commercial printing only in that they printed by one of the commercial processes.

Thermography is raised printing that is heat-induced. The printed images look like engraving.

Forms of printed matter

Most all printed matter can be classified under one of the divisions below. All artists dealing with printing should know the correct names of these forms. You may be asked to design one.

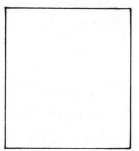

Single leaf is a *leaf* or *sheet*.

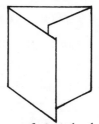

Leaf folded into two or more folds is a *folder*.

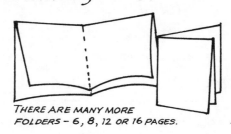

THERE ARE MANY MORE FOLDERS – 6, 8, 12 OR 16 PAGES.

Leaf printed on one side and folded to form 4 pages is a *french fold*.

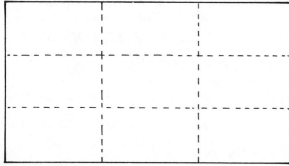

Large leaf folded to make a large, finished folder is a *broadside*.

Book form with paper cover is *booklet* or *pamphlet*. If exquisitely designed it is a *brochure*.

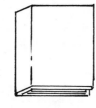

Book form sewn and bound is a *book*. If cover is paper, it is called a *paperback*.

In the case of booklets or book forms the sheets, once folded, are gathered together in order, and the *signatures* (folded sheets) are *collated*. After all the signatures are collated, they are stitched together by either of the two methods shown below.

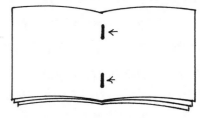

SADDLE STITCH
STAPLES (ARROWS) ARE FORCED THROUGH THE BACKBONE IN THE EXACT CENTER OF THE FOLDED SIGNATURES.

SIDE STITCH
STAPLES ARE FORCED IN SIDE 1/8"– 1/4" FROM BIND SIDE. BOOK CANNOT LIE FLAT WHILE OPENED. COVERS ARE GLUED ON.

Booklets have a final finishing operation called *trimming*. The top and bottom and one side are trimmed with a guillotine paper cutter. In large editions 3 knives are used to trim all 3 sides at once.

Forms of binding

Books and booklets are bound together by one of the processes shown below (if not bound by side-wire or saddle-wire stitching).

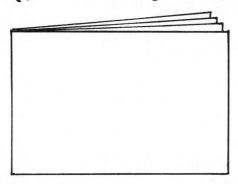

Adhesive binding, ALSO KNOWN AS PERFECT BINDING. PAGES LIE FLAT WHEN OPEN. IT IS NOT A DURABLE BINDING.

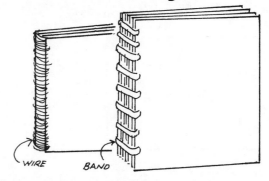

WIRE   BAND

Spiral or mechanical binding. PAGES ARE PUNCHED SO THAT METAL OR PLASTIC WIRES OR BANDS CAN BE WOVEN THROUGH.

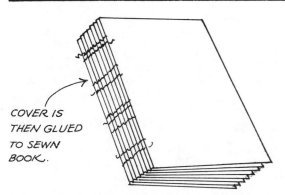

COVER IS THEN GLUED TO SEWN BOOK.

Sewn book. FOLDED SIGNATURES ARE SEWN TOGETHER WITH STRONG THREAD. THIS IS THE MOST COMMON FORM OF BOOKBINDING.

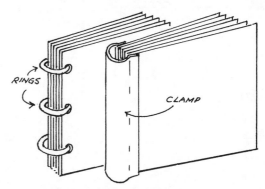

RINGS   CLAMP

Looseleaf binding. PAGES AND COVERS ARE FASTENED TOGETHER WITH CLAMPS OR METAL RINGS.

Other mechanical processes applied to the forms of printed matter are folding, scoring, perforating, diecutting, punching, trimming, embossing, blind stamping, round cornering, drilling, gumming, varnishing, lacquering, and thermography (applying heat to raise the ink). All processes require separate machines and extra costs. Every graphic designer should be completely oriented in them.

Envelopes and mailers

The graphic designer should know the standard envelope forms. If your designed layout is to be mailed, it must fit an envelope, so the design may be affected by the way in which it will be mailed.

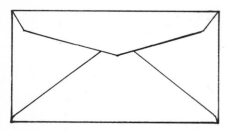

Commercial open side — flap can be sealed (1st class) or tucked in (3rd class)

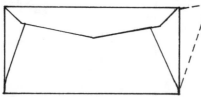

Postage-saver flap can be sealed or unsealed. One end (dotted line) unsealed is 3rd class.

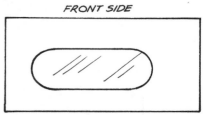

FRONT SIDE

Window — used for statements and invoices.

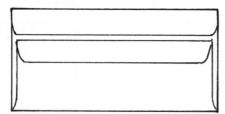

Self-sealing — a time-saver in handling. The flaps have adhesive for instant pressure seal.

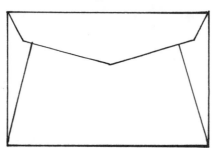

Booklet — open side for direct mail and house organs.

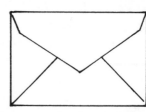

Baronial — fomal deep pointed flap. For invitations, greeting cards, announcements.

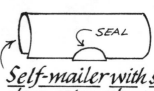

SEAL

Self-mailer with seal — does not need an envelope.

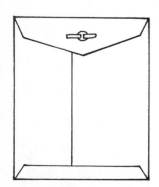

Clasp envelope — flap is closed with metal clasp.

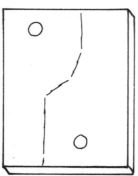

Mailing carton or expansion envelope.

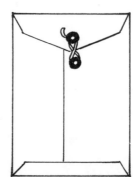

String and button envelope.

BOTH OF THE ABOVE ENVELOPES ARE FOR BULKY ITEMS

LABEL

Mailing tube — ends are sealed or unsealed

Organization
Some tips on organizing your work area

Economy of motion is important to every graphic artist. One way to save time and motion is to keep the things you are working with close to each other and conveniently close to you as you work. If you are using paint or ink and must prepare your brush and later clean it in water, keep your brushes, paint, spread pad, and water supply relatively close together and to the right of your work (if you are right-handed). You invite disastrous results if you have to carry a brush back and forth across your drawing — the paint may dry or you may knock something over or you may drip paint on your work.

Before you leave your work area at night raise your T-square high on the drawing board so that one end of the head does not protrude and "hold it" there with a pushpin. The cleaning person will not hit the head, possibly knocking some materials to the floor.

How a slot cut in your drawing board can help in stripping pieces together

If you have many occasions to strip pieces together in a long continuous strip, a small slot cut in your drawing board may do the job. The slot to the left of your board allows paper strip to slide to the left and down without interfering with the action of your T-square. The hole can be cut with a sharp mat knife or a small pointed saw. The hole should be conveniently positioned on the drawing board so as not to interfere with normal work when not in use.

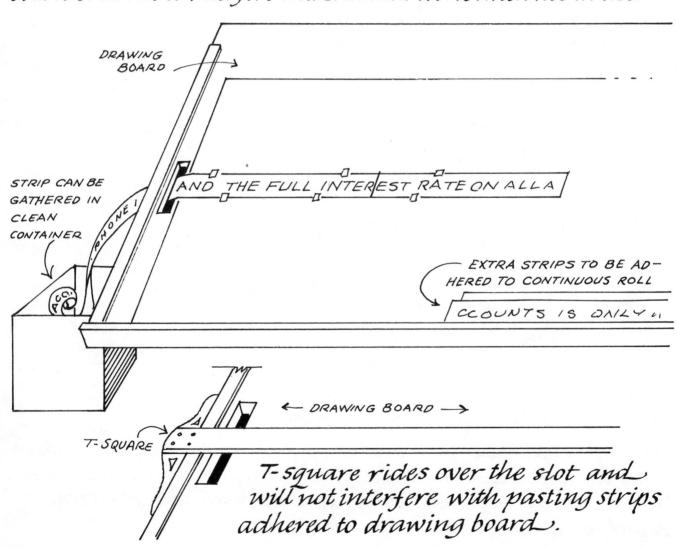

DRAWING BOARD

STRIP CAN BE GATHERED IN CLEAN CONTAINER

PHONE !

AND THE FULL INTEREST RATE ON ALL A

EXTRA STRIPS TO BE ADHERED TO CONTINUOUS ROLL

CCOUNTS IS ONLY 4

← DRAWING BOARD →

T-SQUARE

T-square rides over the slot and will not interfere with pasting strips adhered to drawing board.

How to extend your layout area

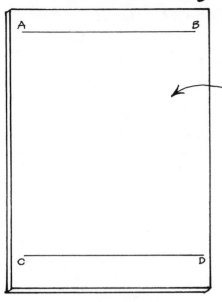

Suppose you have a layout problem. You want to divide the area between lines AB and CD into 26 equal parts. You decide to use the scale method, rotating your ruler until 26 units match points on the 2 lines. You find that a ruler will not fit.

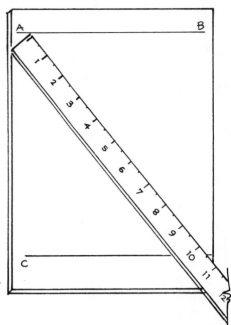

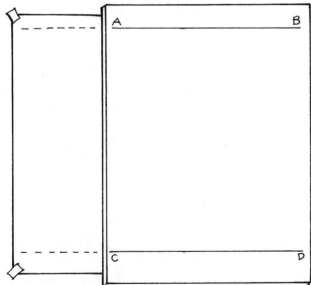

Insert a piece of paper larger than the distance between AB and CD, and extend the lines as shown with dotted lines above. Secure this paper so that it doesn't move as you proceed.

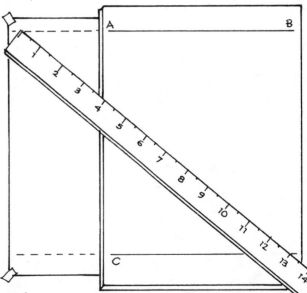

You can now conveniently mark off 26 equal parts (½" each), draw the lines, and proceed with your layout. Extension paper can be discarded.

How to prevent objects from sliding on your board

Did you ever have the questionable thrill of having a large jar of paint slide down your drawing board? To prevent this from happening, paint rubber cement on the bottoms of any objects that may slide.

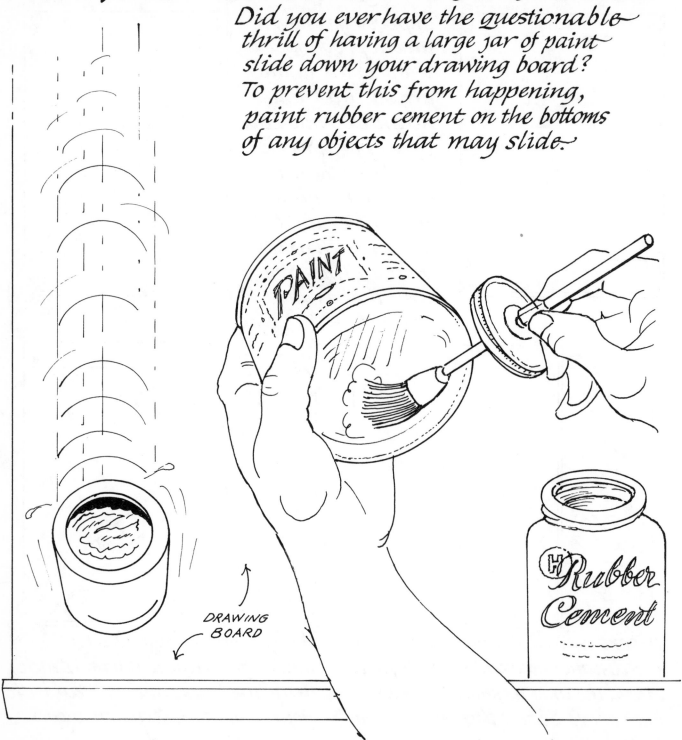

DRAWING BOARD

PAINT

Rubber Cement

Design *and* Color

How to use graph paper as an aid in design

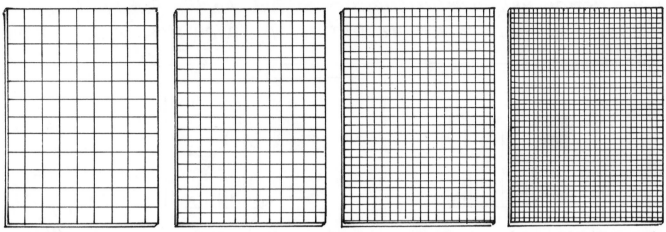

Graph paper can be bought in sheets or pads. It is usually lined with blue lines, will not reproduce if line art (black) is drawn on the graph paper. It comes in many sizes (squares per inch) and can be used for a variety of sized layouts scaled to the sizes of the squares. The paper usually takes writing ink well and thus is good for calligraphy to be reproduced – the blue lines acting as guide lines.

It is great for practicing calligraphy and is inexpensive. It can also be used under tissue or vellum sheets to help align elements of a layout. It can be "positioned" in many angles and taped to sheet underneath.

The quick bro
wwwwn fox
jumped overrr
the lazy dog
aadddgggqq
The queck 12345
Dennis Park.k

GRAPH PAPER

TRACING PAD

How to visualize a design on different backgrounds

In developing a design it is sometimes difficult to imagine what your design will look like against various backgrounds. If the design is in one color or more and in line, follow the directions below.

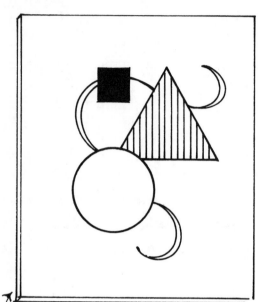 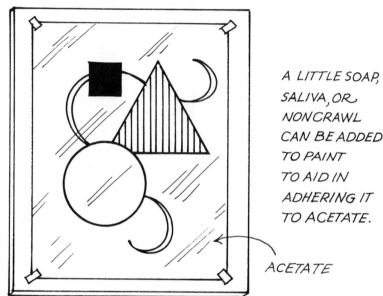

A LITTLE SOAP, SALIVA, OR NONCRAWL CAN BE ADDED TO PAINT TO AID IN ADHERING IT TO ACETATE.

ACETATE

This is your design. Attach it to drawing board, lay a piece of acetate over it, and redraw the design. It doesn't have to be finished art—just enough to represent your design. This acetate drawing can now be laid over different colored backgrounds and patterns so you can evaluate them and reach a decision.

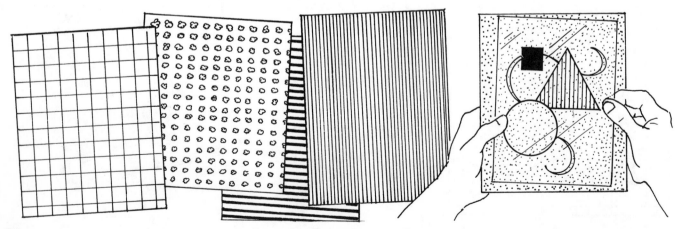

How to make a word stand out in a composition

While the information below is basic, the suggestions may help the designer to emphasize a word in a line. The information relates to other design elements as well as words. Combinations of two or more of the devices are possible.

THE WORD IS **MUM** AND YOU KNOW IT	THE WORD IS **MUM** AND YOU KNOW IT	THE WORD IS *MUM* AND YOU KNOW IT
Make the word *larger*— the style and alignment is the same.	Make the word **bolder**— everything else is the same.	The word is in italic— everything else is in regular roman.
THE WORD IS <u>MUM</u> AND YOU KNOW IT	THE WORD IS **MUM** AND YOU KNOW IT	THE WORD IS MUM AND YOU KNOW IT
Underscore the word or phrase.	Make the word a different color	The word is in a different style of lettering.
THE WORD IS →MUM AND YOU KNOW IT	THE WORD IS MUM AND YOU KNOW IT	THE WORD IS MUM AND YOU KNOW IT
Use a directional device — fingers pointing, arrows, etc.	Isolate the word.	Use a border device or simple outline.

19

How to "eliminate" cut marks on a mechanical

When you are working on a paste-up, mechanical, or any design in which many images are pasted down, it is sometimes difficult to evaluate the design because the shadows of the cut marks around the elements show and it is hard to appraise the relationships.

To minimize these cut marks, making it easier to evaluate your design, hold your paste-up towards a light source so that you are looking at your design in shadow.

Tips on making an effective poster

The most effective posters are those in which the main element of the design is communicated at a glance. This main feature should dominate the card — everything else is subordinated. Some smaller elements can be larger and bolder than other small elements, depending on where you want emphasis. Tell the reader at a glance, immediately, what your poster is all about.

Color and tone contrast can be used to support the dominance of the main element. Allow comfortable margins — let your information breathe. Do not use ornate, hard-to-read styles of lettering. Make it easy on the reader.

Too many conflicting elements confuse — do not convey the message immediately and are hard to read. The poster to the right is bad because it has these faults. Remember — everything doesn't have to be large to invite readership.

ST. JOHN'S HIGH SCHOOL WILL PRESENT THEIR 197• ANNUAL DANCE "FROLIK" ON SATURDAY EVE NOV 10

MUSIC BY TOOTS TEAGUE AND HIS BAND

• FOOD • FOR EVERY ONE o

FIREWORKS AT MIDNIGHT

THERE WILL BE A DRAWING FOR A CAR

BRING THE WHOLE FAMILY

Some notes on color

Volumes have been written on color. Here are a few basic principles.

Warm colors are yellow, orange, and red. They are positive and aggressive, restless and stimulating.

Cool colors are blues, greens, and violets. They are negative and retiring, tranquil and serene.

Color preferences of most people are pure colors in the following order: ① Red, ② Blue, ③ Violet, ④ Green, ⑤ Orange, and ⑥ Yellow.

To deepen, soften, or tone a color, add a little of its complement. For example, a touch of green added to red will deepen or darken the red.

Color mixing. Orange with a touch of ultramarine makes terra-cotta. Yellow with a bit of violet makes olive. Green with a bit of magenta makes myrtle. Turquoise with a touch of red makes peacock blue. Violet with a bit of yellow makes plum. Ultramarine with a touch of orange makes navy blue. Magenta with a bit of green makes claret. Magenta and ultramarine make a great purple, but don't mix ultramarine with vermillion — a muddy and dirty purple. Try not to use black to deepen a color or white to lighten it. Use lighter or darker colors instead.

Colors' "other names". If you don't know what it is, you may find it here:

Pale green – seafoam	Corn – light orange, Persian orange
Dark green – bottle green, forest grn.	
Olive green – emerald green	Orange – tangerine
Dark blue – midnight, gulf, navy	Dark brown – beaver, cocoa
Pea green – tropical green, oriental green	Tan – buff
	Fawn – light brown, sepia
Pale blue – robin's egg	Salmon – coral
Navy blue – marine blue	Maroon – oxblood
Ultramarine – new blue	Pale gray – pearl gray
Yellow – canary, buttercup	Shetland green – dark green

Layout

How to make a device for visualizing your layout

When you are making a layout on a larger (than layout) pad, visualizing what your layout really looks like can be deceptive (because of the surrounding white space). To help you visualize completely what your trimmed layout will look like when it is printed use the device shown below.

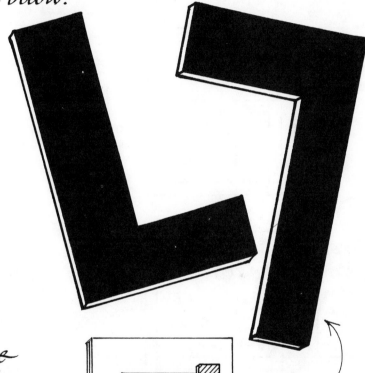

The white space around is like a mat on a framed watercolor. It has a tendency to make your layout look better than it is

Cut 2 large, wide black cardboard pieces as shown on the upper right. Use them as shown here. You may want to make some changes.

LAYOUT

L-SHAPES ARE MADE AS WIDE AND LONG AS YOUR USUAL LAYOUT SIZES.

How to make an aid for drawing repeated layouts

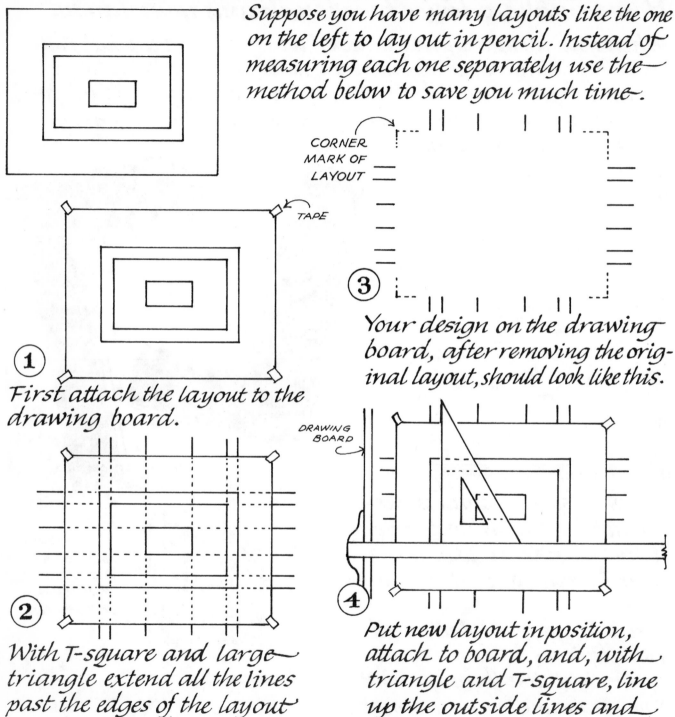

Suppose you have many layouts like the one on the left to lay out in pencil. Instead of measuring each one separately use the method below to save you much time.

CORNER MARK OF LAYOUT

TAPE

① First attach the layout to the drawing board.

② With T-square and large triangle extend all the lines past the edges of the layout (dotted lines above).

③ Your design on the drawing board, after removing the original layout, should look like this.

DRAWING BOARD

④ Put new layout in position, attach to board, and, with triangle and T-square, line up the outside lines and draw in the layout.

How to place images under a layout for tracing

You may have a layout taped to a drawing board and do not want to lift it in order to trace photos or other images. The following aid may help you solve this problem.

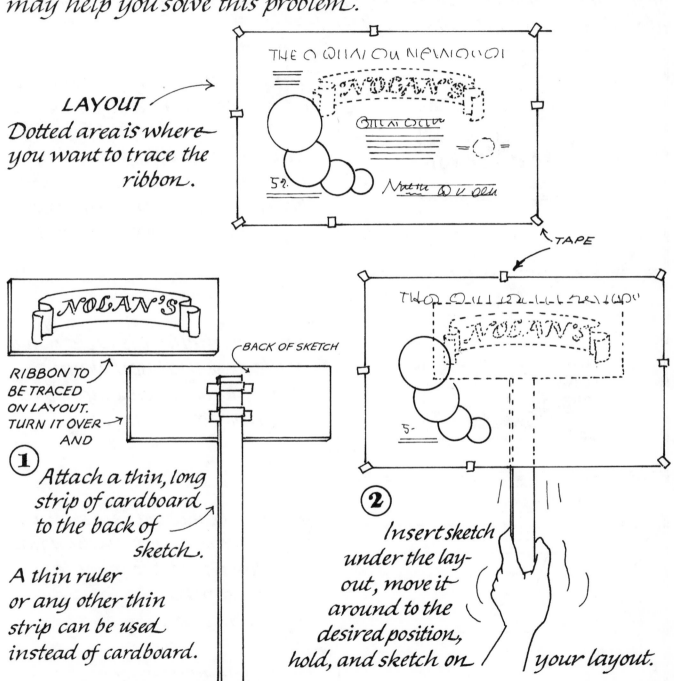

LAYOUT
Dotted area is where you want to trace the ribbon.

TAPE

RIBBON TO BE TRACED ON LAYOUT. TURN IT OVER AND

BACK OF SKETCH

① Attach a thin, long strip of cardboard to the back of sketch.

A thin ruler or any other thin strip can be used instead of cardboard.

② Insert sketch under the lay-out, move it around to the desired position, hold, and sketch on your layout.

How to show crop marks on a photo and other art

Crop marks show the part of a picture that you want the printer to make a plate for. When you show the marks, you want to save the rest of the art for possible future use. <u>Never</u> draw crop marks right on the art. Show them as in the examples below.

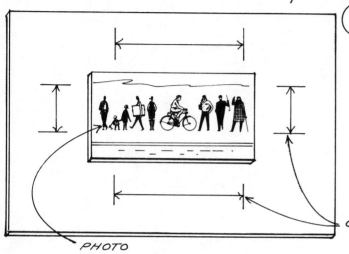

PHOTO

CROP MARKS

① First mount your photo or art (if it does not already have a wide mat of white). In this margin show the area that you want to be printed. The board that it is mounted on will also reinforce the art.

MAT

② Another method is to cut a mat of the area that you want. This may be an odd mat, but it is not for framing.

REGISTER MARKS

CROP HERE

③ Another method is to show the picture area on a vellum flap (don't forget to include register marks for greater accuracy).

NORMALLY THE REGISTER MARKS ARE CLOSER TO THE CROP AREA THAN SHOWN HERE.

How to mount clippings and stretch watercolor paper

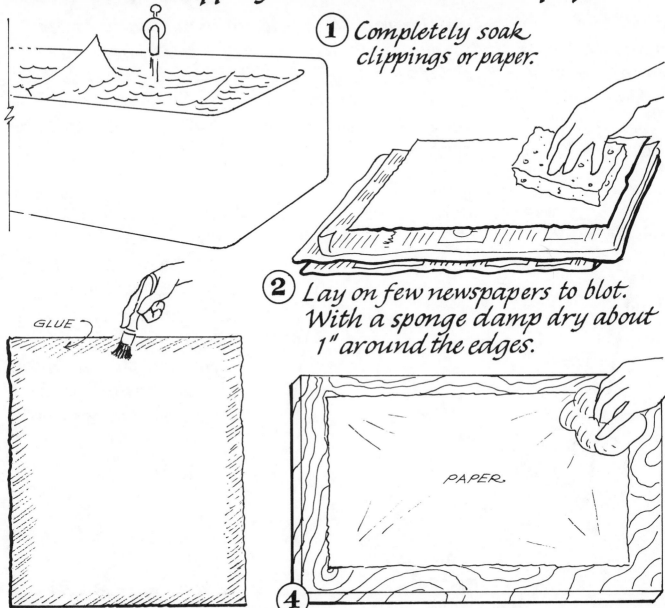

1. Completely soak clippings or paper.

2. Lay on few newspapers to blot. With a sponge damp dry about 1" around the edges.

GLUE

3. Apply glue with a brush about 1" in from the edges.

PAPER

4. Turn paper over and press onto board. Secure it around the edges with paper tape. Staples can be tacked around the edges. The paper will stretch taut when dry.

How to mail or transport a drawing or photo

Never fold or roll a drawing or photo—especially one that is to be reproduced by some printing process. This is especially true if you are going to mail it. If you are mailing it, support the art with cardboard stiffeners and supports, with the art sandwiched in between. The art may crack off, especially if retouched, if you roll it, and fold marks on photos will surely reproduce.

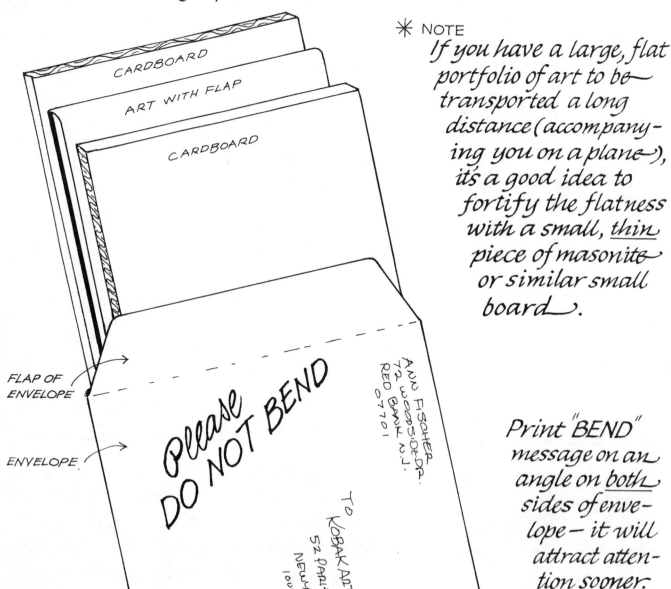

CARDBOARD

ART WITH FLAP

CARDBOARD

FLAP OF
ENVELOPE

ENVELOPE.

Please
DO NOT BEND

ANN FISCHER
72 WOODSIDE DR.
RED BANK N.J.
07701

TO
KOBAK ART
52 PARK
NEWK
10011

✳ NOTE

If you have a large, flat portfolio of art to be transported a long distance (accompanying you on a plane), it's a good idea to fortify the flatness with a small, thin piece of masonite or similar small board.

Print "BEND" message on an angle on both sides of envelope—it will attract attention sooner.

How to draw an aligning line on your drawing board

If you do a lot of work on your drawing board with tissue and vellum sheets, it is a big help to have an aligning line or lines drawn on the surface of your board.

Attach a white card to your drawing board. This is the working surface of the drawing board. To help alignment, draw an aligning line (AB) in a convenient place to help you align translucent items.

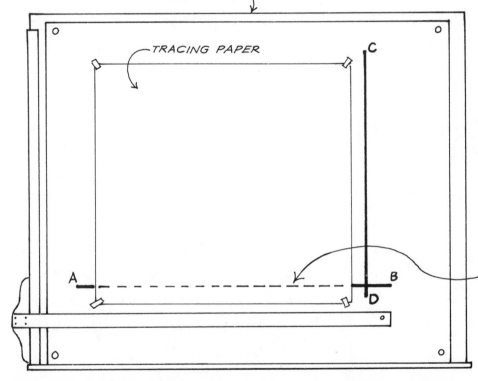

WORKING SURFACE OF BOARD (REPLACEABLE WHITE CARD)

DRAWING BOARD

TRACING PAPER

Other aligning lines can be drawn (CD), but don't draw too many — it will be too confusing.

The lines are also an aid for aligning cards or illustration boards. The dotted line shows the aligning line under the tracing paper.

How to use a paper's edge to check alignment

The straight long edge of a sheet of letter paper can be used to check alignment of elements on a layout.

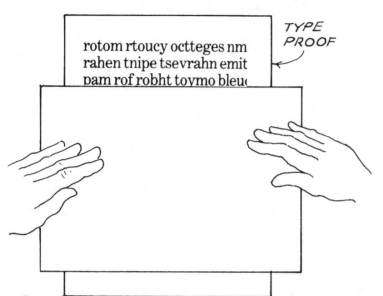

TYPE PROOF

rotom rtoucy octteges nm
rahen tnipe tsevrahn emit
pam rof robht toymo bleu

① The straight edge can be moved to check alignment of all the lines on a type proof.

② It can also be used to check alignment of elements already pasted down on a layout (or mechanical) that cannot be checked with a T-square.

LAYOUT

PARK ZIPS METS

PHILLIES ACE NO-HITS N.Y. LEADERS

IT'S A HIT IN ANY LEAGUE

ZIPPY'S

GOOD FOR WHAT ALES YOU!

ACETATE

③ A piece of acetate with a thin, straight black line drawn on it can also be used to check alignment. It has an advantage over the paper — it is transparent, allowing you to see all the other elements on the layout.

How to use a metal T-square to cut very long cards

Line up the metal top edge of the T-square with the line to be cut on the card. Insert 2 push pins, one at either end of the T-square, so that it will not move as you cut the card with a knife.

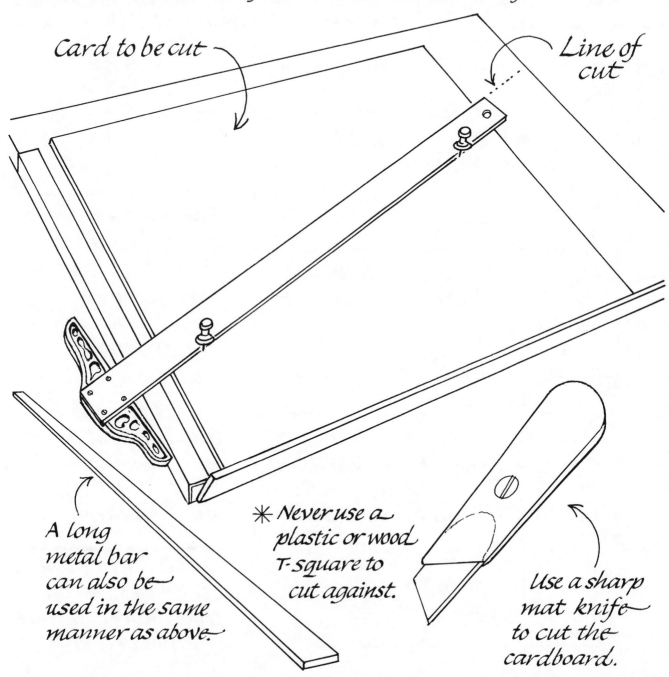

Card to be cut

Line of cut

A long metal bar can also be used in the same manner as above.

※ Never use a plastic or wood T-square to cut against.

Use a sharp mat knife to cut the cardboard.

Corrections and Cleaning
How to prevent smudged ink lines

If you are a careful, neat worker, you will probably have no trouble with wet ink lines when you use a T-square. If you are not, try some of the hints below to keep your drawing or mechanical clean and neat.

① The dash line above represents the pencil line you want to ink in on your mechanical.

② Place a long, thin strip of cardboard near this line but not covering it.

③ Carefully place your T-square over this strip, line up the line, and ink it in. The strip underneath is indicated by the dotted line.

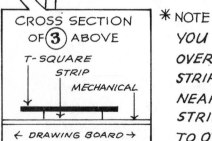

CROSS SECTION OF ③ ABOVE
T-SQUARE
STRIP
MECHANICAL
← DRAWING BOARD →

*NOTE
YOU CAN TURN THE T-SQUARE OVER AND CEMENT A LONG STRIP OF BLOTTING PAPER NEAR (¼") THE INKING EDGE. STRIPS CAN ALSO BE GLUED TO OTHER TOOLS.

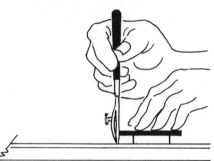

The diagram above shows the position of the inking tool—vertically or at a 90° angle from the drawing surface.

This is the kind of line you will get if you press the ruling pen too hard against the T-square.

This is the line you will get if pen slopes away from drawing surface or is not at a 90° angle.

How to remove tape used to secure art to a board

Whenever tape is used to hold art down on the drawing board or anywhere else, ALWAYS remove it from the inside, or art part, to the outside. NEVER pull tape in towards the art to remove it. If art is on the board you may remove part of a ply (the art side) if you pull the tape toward the art, with disastrous results.

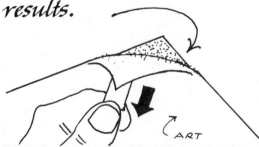

ART

How to correct a black ink line on a white background

If you make a mistake drawing black line art on white illustration board, here is one way to correct it

GRAPFIC

The above lettering was mispelled and the F must be painted out with white paint and changed to an H.

GRAPᴵIC

GRAP IC

The retouched area is sprayed with fixative. This step can be repeated

GRAPHIC

Now paint the new letter.

How to clean out an area in a watercolor painting

It is possible to clean out an area for repainting in a watercolor. Follow the instructions below to have another chance on that watercolor done on that expensive paper.

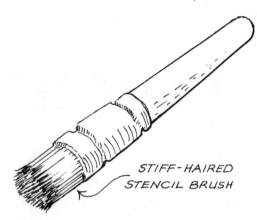

STIFF-HAIRED STENCIL BRUSH

NOTE! DO NOT SCRUB TOO HARD WITH THE BRUSH — YOU MAY DAMAGE THE FIBERS OF THE PAPER.

Suppose that the dotted-line circled area to the right is not correct and you want to change it. Using a stiff stencil brush and lots of clean water, gently scrub the area, agitating the paint. Use a blotter after a moment to blot up the spot. Have lots of blotting paper handy. Repeat the proceedure, using clean blotting paper each time and lots of clean water, and in time you should have a clean area ready for reworking. For sharp-edged areas use a cutout stencil and brush.

How to clean wax from a mechanical

Suppose that you use a waxer instead of rubber cement to adhere elements on to a mechanical and you want to reposition something that is already adhered. You want to file away the piece you remove but you do not want it to stick to other pieces in your file cabinet. The demonstration below should help you solve this problem.

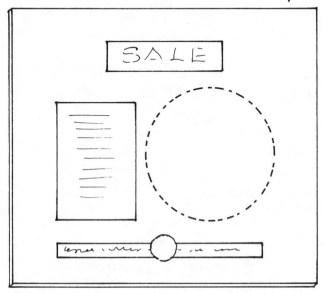

MECHANICAL

The dotted area above is wax left after item has been removed. You now want to clean the area.

With the back end of a metal ruler or the end edge of a small, stiff piece of cardboard scrape the wax off the mechanical. Then clean the area with a wad of cotton and rubber-cement thinner.

Excess wax can be cleaned from the edge of the ruler with your thumbnail.

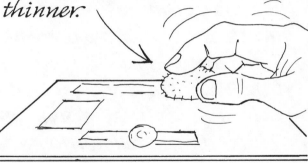

How to remove graphic-art stains from fabrics

A few methods of removing stains are shown below. If there is a question as to what to do, call an expert dry cleaner immediately. These suggestions may help in the meantime.

① Always place absorbent pad under the spot when sponging with solvent.

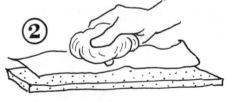

② Sponge with solvent with the spot side down over cloth or blotter.

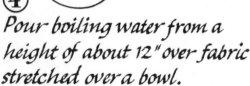

④ Pour boiling water from a height of about 12" over fabric stretched over a bowl.

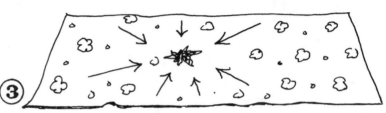

③ Always work from outside in to the center of the spot or stain.

⑤ Always test your reagent on an inconspicuous part of the fabric.

⑥ Never use highly flammable materials such as gasoline or benzene. Friction from rubbing can generate a spark.

⑦ Always rinse all fabrics to remove the reagent.

⑧ Nonflammable solvents (carbon tetrachloride) can be used but they are poisonous, so work in a well-ventilated room, use small quantities, and keep the bottle stoppered while working with it.

⑨ There are 3 kinds of reagents: ① ABSORBENT (cornmeal, dry starch), ② SOLVENTS (water, alcohol, carbon "tet"), and ③ BLEACHES (chlorine, acetic acid solution, white vinegar).

The chart on the following page shows when to use each one.

The chart below shows how to remove different art stains from washable and nonwashable fabrics.

KIND OF STAIN	WASHABLE FABRICS	NONWASHABLE FABRICS
Wax	Scrape off excess with dull knife. Put stained area between 2 blotters and iron with warm iron. If stain remains, sponge with carbon tet or alcohol.	Same as Washable
Dyes	If fabric is white and can be boiled, use commercial color remover (drug store) or bleach with chlorine bleach or hydrogen peroxide. Use bowl or pad method.	Take to expert dry cleaner immediately
Glue	Soak in warm water and launder. If dried, sponge with dilute acetic acid and launder.	Sponge with Carbon tet
Indelible Pencil	Soak in alcohol and launder. If stain remains use chlorine bleach with bowl or pad method.	Take to expert dry cleaner
Ink	While still moist spread with absorbent (cornstarch), brush off and repeat. Launder in warm soap suds. Use commercial ink remover. Soak 1 or 2 days in milk and launder.	Blot up excess and Take to expert dry cleaner
Watercolor Paint	Wash in warm suds	
Oil Paint or Varnish	Sponge with alcohol or carbon tetrachloride.	Sponge with carbon tet or turpentine
Shellac	Soak in equal parts of alcohol and water.	
Alcohol Paints or Stains	Wash in warm suds if fresh or sponge with alcohol. If not fresh, saturate with turpentine and roll up until paint softens. Sponge with more turpentine and launder.	
Wine	Stretch on bowl and cover stain with salt in hot water.	Take to expert dry cleaner
Acrylic Paint	Soak in alcohol and launder	

How to clean rubber-cement stains from mats

Suppose that you are matting pictures or anything else with rubber cement and you have just finished the first one. It's beautiful—except that you accidentally stained the mat with rubber cement. You clean it with a rag and thinner, but the stain is still there. Here is what you do

① *This is the "finished" stained mat. You may want to remove the picture before proceeding.*

② *Spread rubber cement carefully over the entire mat. Do not miss any of the surface, especially the stained areas.*

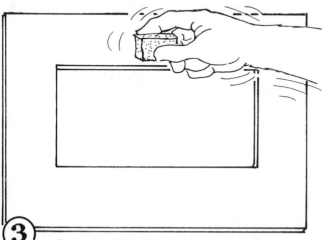

③ *When the rubber cement is dry, remove it with a pickup*

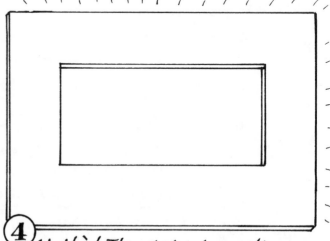

④ *Voilà! The stains have disappeared. This method can, of course, be used in similar situations.*

Copy

How to mark up copy for typesetting (composition)

Accurate markup of copy is a must in the field of typesetting. The typesetter must set it as it is typewritten and marked, so it is very important for all manuscript copy to be correctly marked to minimize errors and keep the cost of composition down. The following is the procedure to be followed by the designer in ordering type.

Paper. Prepare or type your copy on 8½" x 11" white bond with generous borders (for marking your specifications).

Typing should be clean and _double-spaced_. Make a copy in case the original is lost.

Job number. Proper identification – client, address, job number, etc.– should be typed at the top of each sheet.

Numbering. Sheets should be numbered at the top in consecutive order. Mark the end of copy on the last sheet.

Corrections should be made above the line in ink. Never use pencil in giving "specs." Do not write on the back of sheets or attach little notes to the pages. The more correct your specifications, the less costly the _author's_ _alterations_ after the job

Copyfitting. The manuscript copy _must_ fit the layout area according to your specs. This _must_ be checked before ordering type. There are many methods of calculating copy measurement to fit layout – familiarize yourself with this simple procedure.

Markup. The final step is to mark up your copy according to your calculations. All specs must be correct and clear.

How to proofread printed copy

Shown below are standard proofreader's marks, what they mean, and an example of each. They should be learned and used by all who handle type proofs.

MARK	EXPLANATION	EXAMPLE	MARK	EXPLANATION	EXAMPLE
ℓ	TAKE OUT CHARACTER	ℓ The caffrd	⊐	MOVE RIGHT	⊐ The card ǀ
∧	LEFT OUT, INSERT	∧ Te card	‖	ALIGN TYPE	‖ The card / Ace of spa
#	INSERT SPACE	# Thecard	=	STRAIGHTEN LINE	= The card
⊙	TURN INVERTED LETTER	⊙ Tha card	⊙	INSERT PERIOD	⊙ The card∧
eq #	EVEN SPACE	eq # The black card	⌣/	INSERT COMMA	⌣/ The card∧
⌣	LESS SPACE	⌣ The ⌣card	:/	INSERT COLON	:/ The card∧
⌢	CLOSE UP; NO SPACE	⌢ The ccard	;/	INSERT SEMICOLON	;/ The card∧
tr	TRANSPOSE	tr The card red	✓	INSERT APOSTROPHE	✓ The boys card
wf	WRONG FONT	wf The card	⌣⌣ ⌣⌣	INSERT QUOTATION MARKS	⌣⌣ ⌣⌣ Make it∧ card∧
lc	LOWER CASE	lc The Card	=/	INSERT HYPHEN	=/ A card∧mark
sc	SMALL CAPS	sc The card	!	INSERT EXCLAMATION MARK	! What a card∧
c+sc	CAPITALS AND SMALL CAPS.	c+sc The card	?	INSERT QUESTION MARK	? Whose card∧
caps	CAPITALS	caps The card	?	QUERY FOR AUTHOR	? is The card∧dealt
A	CAPITALIZE	C The card	[/]	INSERT BRACKETS	[/] The∧ace∧card
ital	ITALIC	ital The card	(/)	INSERT PARENTHESES	(/) The card∧1∧
rom	ROMAN	rom The card	|1/N|	INSERT 1-EN DASH	|1/N| The card∧
bf	BOLD FACE	bf The card	|1/M|	INSERT 1-EM DASH	|1/M| The card∧
stet	LET IT STAND	stet The card	|2/M|	INSERT 2-EM DASH	|2/M| The card∧
out sc	OUT, SEE COPY	out sc He∧ card	□	INDENT 1-EM	□ The card
spell out	SPELL OUT	spell out King (Geo.)	⊏⊐	INDENT 2-EMS	⊏⊐ The card
¶	START PARAGRAPH	¶ out.∧The card	ld >	INSERT LEAD BETWEEN LINES	ld> The card was dealt by Hal
⌐	RAISE	⌐ The card	hr #	INSERT HAIR SPACE	hr # The card w∧as
⌊	LOWER	⌊ The card	ℓ	DELETE AND CLOSE UP	ℓ The boy's card
⊏	MOVE LEFT	⊏ ǀ The card	Qu?	IS THIS RIGHT?	Qu? The red card

40

The best time to correct or edit copy is before it leaves the shop for the compositor. When correcting proofs use a dark blue, or sharp red line, to clearly show the errors. Make all the corrections in the margins of the proof. Make a vertical line, /, through a wrong letter. Cross out the word to be changed with a horizontal line. Shown below is a corrected proof with most of the common errors.

It does not appear that the earliest printers had any method of correcting errors before the form was on the press. The learned The learned correctors of the first two centuries of printing were not proof readers in our sense, they were rather what we should term office editors. Their labors were chiefly to see that the proof corresponded to the copy, but that the printed page was correct in its latinity—that the words were there, and that the sense was right. They cared but little about orthography, bad letters or purely printers errors, and when the text seemed to them wrong they consulted fresh authorities or altered it on their own responsibility. Good proofs in the modern sense, were impossible until professional readers were employed / men who had first a printer's education, and then spent many years in the correction of proof. The orthography of English, which for the past century has undergone little change, was very fluctuating until after the publication of Johnson's Dictionary, and capitals, which have been used with considerable regularity for the past 80 years, were previously used on the miss or hit plan. The approach to regularity, so far as we have, may be attributed to the growth of a class of professional proof readers, and it is to them that we owe the correctness of modern printing. More errors have been found in the Bible than in any other one work. For many generations it was frequently the case that Bibles were brought out stealthily, from fear of governmental interference. They were frequently printed from imperfect texts, and were often modified to meet the views of those who publised them. The story is related that a certain woman in Germany, who was the wife of a Printer, and had become disgusted with the continual assertions of the superiority of man over woman which she had heard, hurried into the composing room while her husband was at supper and altered a sentence in the Bible, which he was printing, so that it read Narr instead of Herr, thus making the verse read "And he shall be thy fool" instead of "and he shall be thy lord." The word not was omitted by Barker, the king's printer in

How to make a scale for character counting when "specing" type

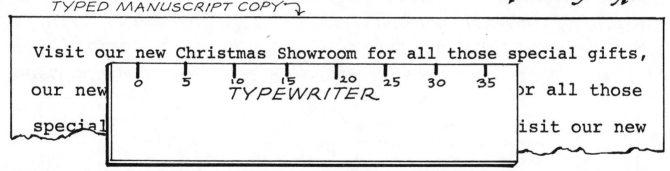

TYPED MANUSCRIPT COPY

Visit our new Christmas Showroom for all those special gifts,

our new ... TYPEWRITER ... or all those

special ... isit our new

0 5 10 15 20 25 30 35

On a piece of card (5"x2" or any size you need) mark off on one side, in divisions of 5, the character count of the typewriter type used in the copy you are about to specify. Lay the edge of the card parallel to the type-written copy to count the characters. Label it "TYPEWRITER."

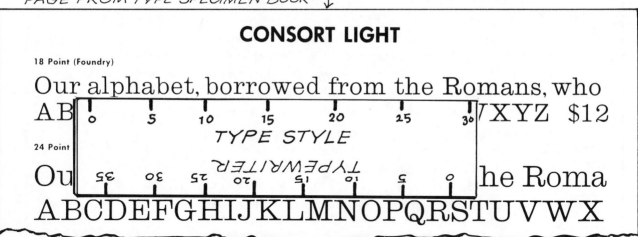

PAGE FROM TYPE SPECIMEN BOOK

CONSORT LIGHT

18 Point (Foundry)

Our alphabet, borrowed from the Romans, who

AB ... VXYZ $12

24 Point

Ou ... he Roma

ABCDEFGHIJKLMNOPQRSTUVWX

0 5 10 15 20 25 30   TYPE STYLE   TYPEWRITER   35 30 25 20 15 10 5 0

Turn the card around and mark the other edge with the character count of the type you have selected for your layout. Mark this side "TYPE STYLE." You can now easily manipulate this card on your layout (to check how many characters of the type will fall on a line) with the character count on your typewritten copy. You may want to save these cards for later use. If you use a few particular type styles often, you will find these cards very helpful.

How to distinguish typefaces by lower case "g"

In learning the distinguishing characteristics of typefaces in order to easily recognize them the one letter that is most often different in different alphabets is the lowercase "g". Learn to look for it - it will help you identify the type.

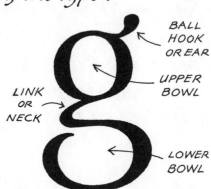

BALL HOOK OR EAR

UPPER BOWL

LINK OR NECK

LOWER BOWL

Study the ball hook at the top of the upper bowl. Notice how large the upper bowl is in relation to the lower bowl. Notice how the lower bowl is joined to the upper bowl.

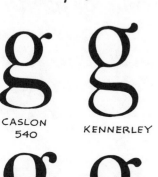

CASLON 540

KENNERLEY

BODONI

CASLON OLD FACE

GARAMOND

JENSON

P.T. BARNUM

FRANKLIN GOTHIC EXTRA COND.

FUTURA MEDIUM

MARY ANN

FUTURA BLACK

FUTURA BOLD CONDENSED

GOUDY BOLD

CALEDONIA

LEGEND

GOUDY TEXT

LYDIAN BOLD COND.

OPTIMA SEMI BOLD

PRETORIA

CENTURY EXPANDED

CONTACT BOLD

CASLON BLACK

TIMES ROMAN

BULLETIN TYPE-WRITER

CELTIC

STYMIE BOLD

HEROLD REKLAME

EURO-STILE

NEWS GOTHIC EXTRA COND.

ADONIS EXTENDED

How to letter-space, word-space, and line-space

Spacing type or lettering is a matter of eye judgment. The "rules" below will help you develop this sense. Lettering is demonstrated, but the same "rules" of legibility apply to type.

Letter space is the area between letters of a word from top guideline (cap line) to bottom line (base or aligning line). These areas are easy to evaluate when the edges of the letters are vertical, biased, or elliptical from top to bottom. For the open-sided letters such as C, E, Z, etc. judge ½ of the inside space to the adjacent letter to figure your area.

INVOCIZTIO — CAP LINE / BASE LINE

Assuming that the letters above form a word, all the cross-hatched areas should look the same (equal in area) to the eye – 2 straights, as in "IN" above, are farthest apart, and 2 curves (OC) are closest. Letter space is the same throughout the entire copy – no matter how many lines.

Word space is the space between words in continuous copy – can be different but not vastly different – in order to align the right hand margin.

THE QUICK BROWN FOX
JUMPS OVER LAZY DOGS

In the drawing above word space is the shaded area between words. Normal word space is the width of the letter "c."

Line space is the white space between lines of lettering or type (shaded part below). The distances from base line to base line are equal. Never have more word space than line space.

THE QUICK BROWN FOX
PACKED THREE DOZEN
JUGS BEFORE HE 334
JUMPED OVER THE 56
LAZY DOGS.

← Base lines

44

How to prepare a porous surface for painting

Blotters, cloth, and other porous materials can be prepared with a spray to minimize bleeding of colors. In the case of T-shirts, for example, stretch the material, spray it with workable or other fixative (varnish), and paint your image. The color may still bleed — but not as much.

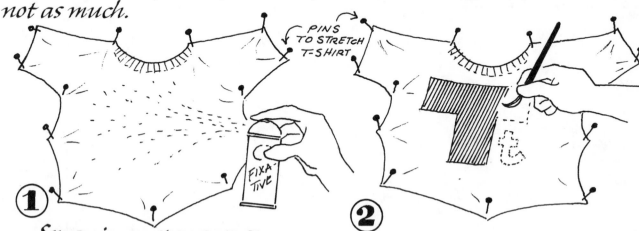

PINS TO STRETCH T-SHIRT

FIXATIVE

① Spray in an open area so that you will not breathe the fixative – outdoors, in a closed room with a fan blowing out, in a window, etc.

② Sketch first in pencil and then paint your design. Color used should be waterproof in this instance.

MASK

An interesting effect can be achieved by masking out areas with a blotter or similar porous material, and painting over the entire area. Masked area will have a slightly different value.

How to paint on shiny and/or glossy surfaces

Any graphic artist knows what a bother it is to paint watercoler or tempera on top of glossy photographs or glossy varnished reproduced art. He invariably has trouble making the paint adhere and <u>stay</u> on the glossy surface. Here are some suggestions that will eliminate this problem.

1 Gently erase over the shiny surface with a kneaded eraser.

3 Gently spray over the glossy area before and after painting. Use workable fixative.

FIXATIVE

2 Noncrawl is a solution especially prepared for mixing with color to aid in painting on glossy surfaces.

NON CRAWL

SOAP

Soap or saliva mixed with paint will also help paint adhere to glossy surfaces.

PAINT

SPREAD CARD

How to dry wet art and photos quickly

An invaluable tool in every art and photography studio is a regular hair dryer. It will save so much time that the cost of buying is not prohibitive.

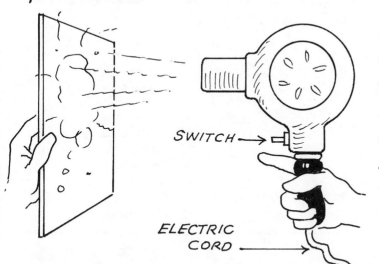

Hold the dryer away from the art or photo. Warm air is blown against the art almost instantaneously. Do not hold too close – you may blur heavily inked lines. Photo prints and photostats can be dried in seconds. Some watercolor artists use the dryer to save precious working time.

SWITCH →

ELECTRIC CORD →

How to make your design more transluscent

You may want your design to be more transluscent – for tracing or photographic purposes. Put your art face down on clean surface and, with a cotton ball or soft rag, spread mineral oil over the back of your sketch. Be sure to clean off all the excess oil with clean rags when you have finished.

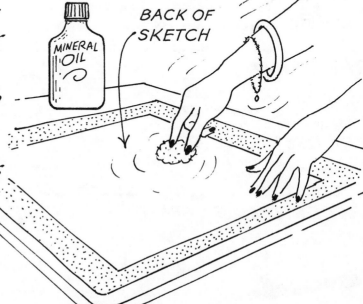

MINERAL OIL

BACK OF SKETCH

Do-it-yourself Silkscreen
How to make your own silkscreen set-up

Silkscreen (screen process) is a stencil method of printing posters, prints, wallpaper, T-shirts – just about anything. Below are the parts, and on the next page is the technique.

The FRAME

4 PIECES OF WOOD, 2 EACH OF 2 LENGTHS, 2" X 3" IN THICKNESS, ARE ATTACHED AT CORNERS.

THE CORNERS CAN BE BRACED WITH FLAT METAL ANGLES.

A PIECE OF SILK IS ATTACHED TO FRAME, WHICH IS TURNED OVER, ANGLE SIDE DOWN.

SILK CAN BE STAPLED OR TACKED IN THE SEQUENCE SHOWN ABOVE. ARROWS SHOW DIRECTION OF PULL AS YOU ATTACH.

The STENCIL

WITH TUSCHE INK YOUR DESIGN CAN BE PAINTED RIGHT ON STRETCHED SILK. GLUE, THEN SPREAD ALL OVER, AND, WHEN DRY, REMOVE TUSCHE WITH WASH OF KEROSENE.

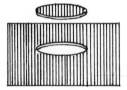

BROWN KRAFT PAPER CAN BE CUT AND ATTACHED TO SCREEN WHEN STENCIL IS CUT.

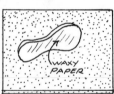

AMBER LACQUER FILM (2 PLY) CAN BE CUT AND ADHERED WITH LACQUER THINNER.

STENCILS CAN BE MADE PHOTOGRAPHICALLY.

The PAINT

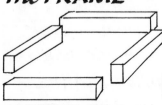

WATERCOLOR CAN BE USED IF THE STENCIL IS WATER-REPELLENT, AS IN THE LACQUER-BASED FILM.

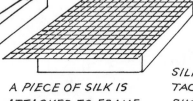

CANS OF SPECIAL FINE-GROUND SCREEN PAINT CAN BE BOUGHT. THEY ARE OIL-BASED.

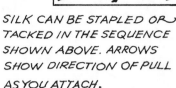

LACQUER AND ENAMEL PAINTS ARE USED FOR WOOD, METAL, GLASS, ETC.

ACCESSORIES

RUBBER SQUEEGEE

TURPENTINE AND KEROSENE THINNERS

LIQUID GLUE FOR BLOCKOUT

TAPE FOR SEALING CORNERS

SMALL CARDS FOR REGISTERING

PAPER AND CARDS TO PRINT ON

Silkscreen printing

After the frame is built, the silk stretched, the stencil made and adhered to the screen, the paint mixed, and the paper stacked conveniently for printing you are ready to print.

CLOTHESLINE FOR HANGING PRINTS TO DRY

STRONG SPRING

PAPER OR CARDS

HINGES

HINGE CLAMP

The screen (plate) is lowered and held down. Paint (buttery texture) is added to one end of the screen. The squeegee carries the paint across the stencil and prints onto the paper, which you have positioned against the register marks on the baseboard before lowering the screen. After printing the print is hung on the clothesline to dry. Put the next sheet of paper on the baseboard against the register marks, lower the screen, and squeegee the paint across the stencil, this time in the reverse direction. Continue the operation until all the papers are printed. Clean the screen with proper paint thinner and tools (squeegee), and you are ready for your next job.

The post setup shown at top is fine, but you need only a strip of wood on the edge of the frame to hold the screen up. It can be kicked to lower the screen with your left hand.

FRAME →

SCREW WITH LARGE HOLE IN STICK

HINGE CLAMP

BASE

SIDE VIEW

How to print blended color by silkscreen

Beautiful blended-color effects are possible with silkscreen, as described below.

With the screen in a slightly elevated position, deposit small amounts of pastelike color (not too thin) side by side at the inside-hinge end of the screen. Plan your color sequence and have all your colors mixed before depositing them on the screen. They can be deposited with tongue depressors, one for each color, which can be thrown away later. If paint is to come to edge of paper (cropped when dry), you must allow for this extra paper - which is larger than trim will be. With paper or card in position on baseboard, move squeegee back and forth across your screen in an oscillating motion and print your color. The first prints may be streaky, but streaks will eventually disappear.

Do not turn squeegee around as you continue printing. Work fast and you should get 20+ prints before cleaning and doing more. Cleaned-off paint can be saved, mixed, and used again as a neutral color on another job.

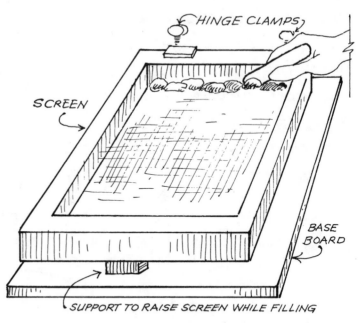

HINGE CLAMPS

SCREEN

BASE BOARD

SUPPORT TO RAISE SCREEN WHILE FILLING

NEVER BRING SCREEN TO A VERTICAL POSITION

SQUEEGEE

PAPER

Lettering

How to identify regular, condensed and extended letter proportions

The lettering on the inscription of the Trajan Column in Rome (113 AD) has established the criteria for the most beautiful letter proportions (width to height of individual letters and letters to each other) for centuries. Here are some of those letter proportions.

ROMANVS

Everyone concerned with the design or use of letters or type should study these letters (on the inscription) as the ideal for the classic form. All alphabets designed since then are regular. Deviations — making them wider (extended) or narrower (condensed) — of the designed alphabet should be understood.

NORMAL
This is one letter of a designed alphabet. It would be the normal set (width to height relationship)

CONDENSED
The same letter (style and height remaining the same). This would be the condensed form of that alphabet. All the other letters of the normal alphabet would also be narrower than normal.

EXTENDED
The same letter (style and height remaining the same). This would be the expanded or extended form of the alphabet.

Design your own style of alphabet and then design a condensed and an extended version. The only letter that remains the same in all three versions is the letter "I."

How to distinguish between blackletter, text, Old English, sans serif, and Gothic letter styles

The above terms have confused designers and students of lettering for a long time. The descriptions below will help you understand the differences.

The more easily understood names for these styles are

Blackletter

For many centuries (10th – 13th) this was the true gothic letter. The Goths had left the scene long before, but the lettering was used on Gothic architecture and was called "Gothic." In northern Europe it was compressed and angular. In southern Europe it was softer, slightly expanded, and more curvilinear. It was very black on the page — so "blackletter" describes it more accurately than Gothic. It was also used for text types in the first printing (Gutenberg Bible). It is sometimes called "Text" in type terminology because of this. Old English is simply another name for Blackletter. The capitals are very decorative; and the style is used frequently today on formal announcements, certificates and religious printing.

sans serif

means what it says — without serifs. American typographers called it Gothic — for what reason no one knows. Perhaps because it remotely resembles Blackletter (Gothic). Some typeface names, mostly American, are Alternate Gothic, News Gothic, etc., but are no more "Gothic" than script, for example. In Europe it is sometimes called "Grotesk".

Futura type (designed by Paul Renner in Germany around 1928) is based on classic proportions. It is still a much used style. It is simple and unadorned. Many distorted forms of it appear in type specimen books. "Gothic" is a misnomer for this style.

Difference between written and built-up lettering

All lettering can be classified under 2 types by method of accomplishing the lettering – written and built-up. The differences are shown below.

Informal Script
> This lettering is freely written with a pen or brush and is done directly – what you write is the lettering. It can be retouched.

Brush
> This style is done with a brush, pointed or flat-edged. It can be retouched.

Calligraphy
> Calligraphic writing is done with a flat-edged tool and the result is immediately finished lettering. It should not be retouched.

All the above lettering is <u>written</u>. There are, of course, many variations of the styles.

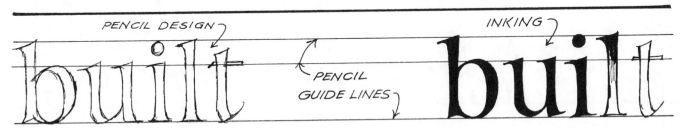

PENCIL DESIGN

INKING

built

PENCIL GUIDE LINES

built

<u>Built-up</u> letters are first carefully designed in pencil and corrected until they are just what you want. Then the letters are carefully outlined in ink, using a pen or brush, and filled in (made solid black) with a brush (usually). They are retouched – first with ink and then with white opaque watercolor – with a brush.

How to write calligraphy

There have been many books written on calligraphy – its historical development, how-to, etc. The remarks below are very basic, and the information is presented simply to get someone who wants to write it started. This is only one form. It has many variations. To do it reasonably well is self-motivating, and anyone with a real _desire_ to write it _can_.

ASCENDER →

DESCENDER →

45°

9°

The height of the capitals is 7 pen widths.

Main body of small letters (minuscule) is 5 pen widths high. Ascenders and descenders are also 5 pen widths.

Edge of pen is held at a 45° angle to the writing line.

Use thin writing ink.

Letters of a word can join.

Slant of letters is 9° (approximately).

Maximum and minimum width of line is attained at right angles.

Basic letter form and same form written with a flat pen.

There is a generally condensed, packed feeling to the lettering. Do not make the letters wide – they will look awkward.

abcdefghijklmnopqrstuv

WXYZ

Practice!
Practice!
Practice!

6 AND 8 AND SOMETIMES 2 ARE ABOVE TOP ALIGNING LINE.

1234567890

3, 5, 7, AND 9 ARE BELOW THE BASE LINE.

ABCCDEFGHIJKLMN
OPQRSTUVWXYYZ

Basic calligraphic forms for capitals. When the situation permits, capitals can have flourishes but not too many in a phrase. The beginning and the end of a sentence are where the flourishes are used most frequently.

The quick brown fox jumps over the.

PENS OR PENCILS ARE SECURED TOGETHER.

You can build up interesting letters with 2 pencils or pens held so that an imaginary line joining their points would be at a 45° angle to the aligning line.

With some retouching and filling in beautiful calligraphic-type letters are possible, as in the example of the minuscule g to the left.

SKETCH   SKETCH REFINED   FILLED IN AND RETOUCHED

How to use swash letters in design

Swashes are the flourished parts of letters and are used mostly at the beginning or ending of a word or phrase.

A E N e e h n

The letters sketched above are swash letters. They are used to add a note of decoration to an otherwise plain phrase as in the example below.

The quick brown

NORMAN Clothes
123

They add a note of distinction, if used properly, to a logotype or trade mark.

NORMAN

If you use too many, they may not communicate the message quickly. One or two letters are most effective.

Never use them in the middle of a word or phra

Optical illusions in lettering

When you letter words, phrases, or simply letters in design, you must be aware of the illusions that occur with letters and how you can compensate for them to make the lettering look right. This is true for rough, comprehensive, or finished lettering. These are the essential illusions.

Parts of letters that have points must come beyond the guide-lines, or they will look too short.

All curves of letters must go beyond the guide-lines, or they will look smaller.

On block letters certain parts, such as those above, must be drawn wider than the down-stroke thickness.

On some letters the outside down strokes should converge toward points so that white space can be drawn and letters will not get spotty as in circled parts of letter to the right.

In block letters the horizontals are slightly thinner than the verticals so that they look like they are the same weight as shown above.

The vertical strokes of capitals are heavier than the verticals of lowercase. If they are drawn with the same weight, the cap width will appear to be thinner.

In slanted italics and scripts, the oval parts of letters tilt at a different direction than the down stroke. Otherwise they will look awkward as in the example above.

How to design an ornamental letter

Ornamental letters are basically letters with decorative effects, as shown below. They should always read, although some letters have histori-cally been difficult to read because of the heavy ornamentation. They are normally used for short words or phrases — if used in excess, they are hard to read because they call attention to themselves and conse-quently are difficult to comprehend. The usual styles of ornament-ation are shown below.

A *Basic letter*	 *Simple outline*	 *Simple shading and outline*	 *Inline and outline*
 *Decorate around the letter*	 *Decorate within the letter*	 *Distort the form of the basic letter*	 *Decorate half the letter*
 *Add pictorial matter*	 *Form the letter with pictorial illustration*	 *Some letters are decorative as in Spencerian*	 *Combinations of 2 or more of the other ideas*

Below are shown some letters as they were developed in the past. Study them to see how the ideas on the other page are exploited. There are many books on decorative and ornamental letters. Study them, then try some of your own. If you are actually going to use one, try to put significant decorative matter on your letter. If you are going to use your letter for a beer ad, for example, the decorative matter may be wheat, malt, barrels, etc.

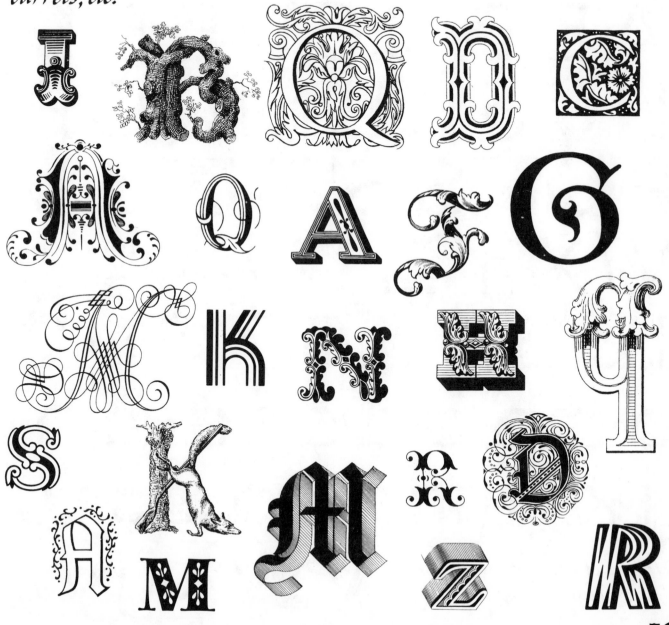

How to letter single stroke letters with a B speedball pen

Below is a demonstration of how to letter single-stroke vertical letters using a B Speedball pen. The light line boxes around the capital letters show the width of the letter in relation to a square. The numbers and arrows show the sequence and direction of strokes.

With the exception of "one," all numbers are almost the same width.

Not a circle

Height of body of lowercase is ⅔ of height of capitals.

How to use the side of a pointed brush and an old ruling pen to letter

Brush before and after pressure

The side of the point of a pointed brush can be used, with practice, to do distinctive lettering, as in the sample below.

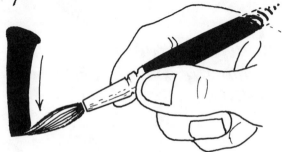

An old ruling pen can be ground down on a sharpening stone to get an edge like this

Apply slight pressure at the beginning of the stroke to get an interesting effect.

Ink or paint can be used. Observe lettering in printed matter that is obviously brush lettering and try to duplicate it. You will eventually develop a personal style.

The pen can be dipped directly into ink and used as a writing pen. Keep the slant the same for most of the lettering, changing only for cross-bars on a t, for example. Again, as in brush lettering, practice, practice, practice and you should eventually develop a personal style.

THANKSGIVING *Friends*

61

How to relate numbers to caps and lower case

1234567890

These are lining or modern number styles. The upper and lower guide lines contain all the numbers – no parts come above or below.

OPTIONAL

1234567890

These are nonaligning or old-style numbers. Even numbers* extend above the top line. Odd numbers come below the bottom guideline. The numbers 1 and 0 are within the guidelines.

* 4 IS EXCEPTION

SALE

LATEST FROM
~ PARIS ~

15% OFF

JUNIOR MISSES
DRESSES

$89.50

When _applicable_ in _your_ designs, try to relate old-style numbers with lower-case letters and modern numbers with capitals – there is an affinity of old style with lowercase (up and down) and modern numbers with all caps as is obvious, in the examples shown here.

Come to ye olde Church Partie
on
31st of May
at
5678 st NW

For benefit of
Children Fund

How to find the center between two points quickly

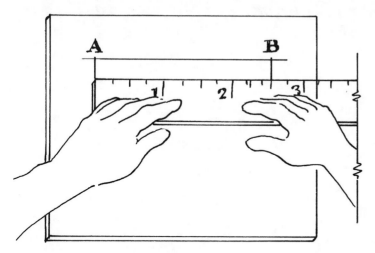

Suppose that you wanted to find the center between points A and B on the sketch to the left. Instead of putting the zero of your ruler at point A, and measuring the actual distance to B, and then dividing it, which gets involved with fractions, do this ↴

Move your ruler left and right until you get a convenient equal distance between numbers (in inches). For example, the ruler measures exactly ¼" from the 1" mark to the left and ¼" from the 3" mark to the right so that the 2" mark would be the center.

With a little practice this method will save you a lot of time.

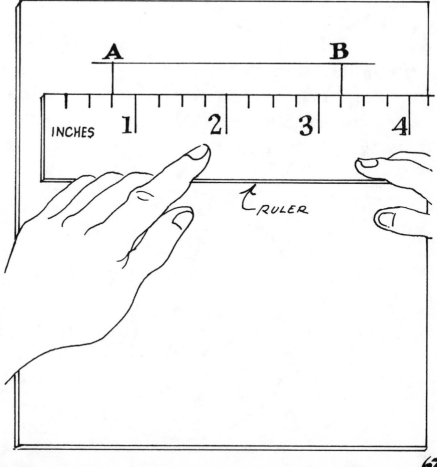

How to find the center of any circle

A chord is a straight line that cuts through any part of a circle at 2 points. Suppose that you have a circle and want to find the center of it.

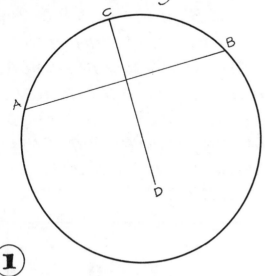

① First draw a chord (AB), divide it in half, and draw a perpendicular line (CD) through this center, as above.

② Draw any other chord (EF) on the same circle, as above. Find the center of this chord and draw a perpendicular line (GH)

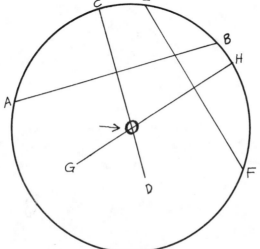

③ Where these two perpendiculars, CD and GH, intersect is the center of the circle (O).

How to divide any distance between lines into any number of equal spaces

In the diagram below let AB and CD be the parallel lines, and AC or BD the distance...

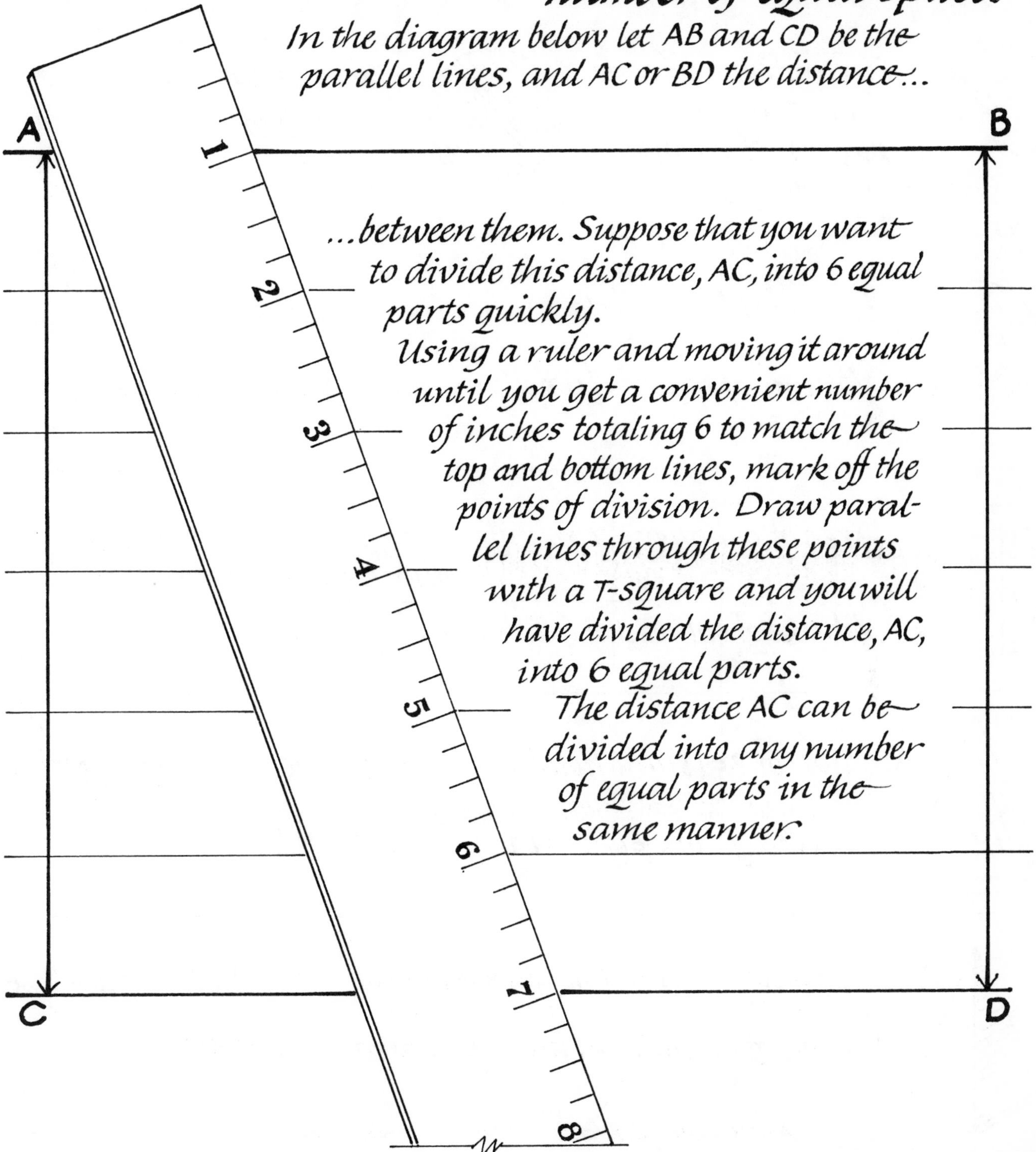

A   B

...between them. Suppose that you want to divide this distance, AC, into 6 equal parts quickly.

Using a ruler and moving it around until you get a convenient number of inches totaling 6 to match the top and bottom lines, mark off the points of division. Draw parallel lines through these points with a T-square and you will have divided the distance, AC, into 6 equal parts.

The distance AC can be divided into any number of equal parts in the same manner.

C   D

Formulas

Here are some formulas for circular forms and a pyramid.

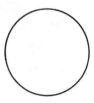 Circumference of circle is the diameter times pi (π). Pi is 3.14159265 or 3.1416.

 Area of circle = diameter x 0.7854, or πr^2.

 Area of sphere (surface) = (radius^2 x 3.1416) x 4.

Volume of sphere = [(radius x radius x radius x π) x 4] ÷ 3.

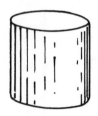 Area of cylinder = circumference of top (or base) x height plus areas of top and base.

Volume of cylinder = (radius^2 x π) x height.

 Area of cone = (slant height x circumference) ÷ 2 + area of base.

Volume of cone = (altitude x area of base) ÷ 3.

 Area of pyramid = (slant height x perimeter of base) ÷ 2 + area of base.

Volume of pyramid = (altitude x area of base) ÷ 3.

WATCH WHERE THOSE DECIMAL POINTS GO!

How to draw an involute (spiral curve)

An involute is a spiral curve. The involute of any polygon may be drawn by extending its sides (as in the two examples below) and, with the corners of the polygon as successive centers, drawing arcs that terminate on the extended sides.

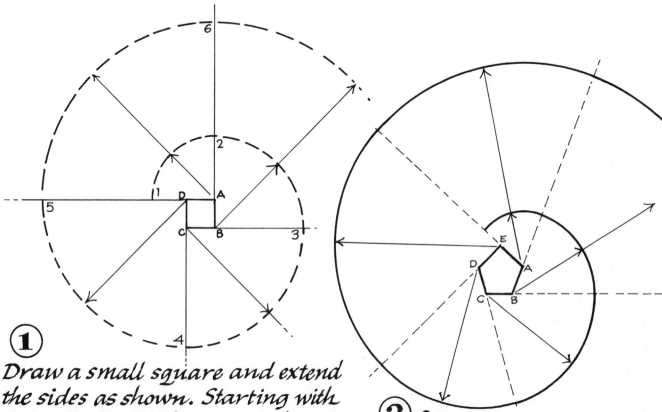

① Draw a small square and extend the sides as shown. Starting with A as a center and A1 as a radius, draw a quarter of a circle, 12. With B as a center and B2 as a radius, draw arc 23. With C as a center and C3 as a radius, draw arc 34. With D as a center and D4 as a radius, draw arc 45. With A as a center and A5 as a radius, draw arc 56 and continue as long as you wish.

② Construct a pentagon ABCDE. Extend the sides as before — these will form the sections where the arcs will meet with A, B, C, D and E as centers, as with the square. Proceed to draw the involute. You can draw involutes with any regular-sided figure.

How to construct an ellipse by the trammel method

Let AB be the major axis, and CD the minor axis.

They intersect at point O.

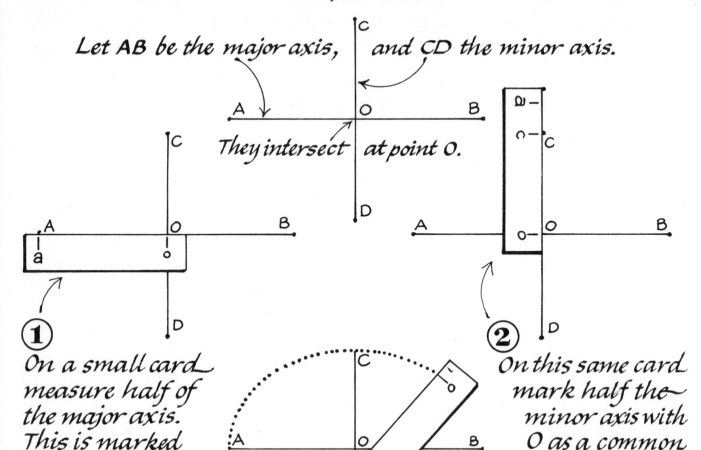

① On a small card measure half of the major axis. This is marked oa on the card above.

② On this same card mark half the minor axis with O as a common mark. On the card this is shown above as oc.

③ You should now have a card that looks like this.

④ On the intersecting axis move this card around to establish all the points on your ellipse. Point a must always be on the <u>minor</u> axis, and the point c must always be on the <u>major</u> axis. Mark the points where o occurs to establish your ellipse.

A machine called an "ellipsograph" is constructed on this same principle.

How to draw a *FAT* 5-pointed star

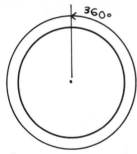

There are 360° in any circle.

A protractor is an instrument for measuring angles. To find 5 equidistant points on the circumference of circle, divide 360° by 5 to get 72°. Using the protractor, you can now get the 5 points on the circle to establish the star.

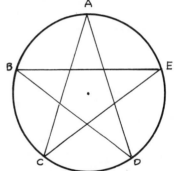

A 5-pointed star has 5 equidistant points, A, B, C, D, and E, on the circumference of a circle. These points must be established on the circle before you can draw a star.

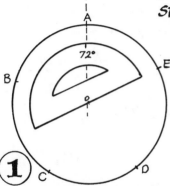

① First draw a circle and mark off, with protractor, the 5 points, each at a 72° angle from the center.

② Draw the lines as shown to get your star.

③ Now find the centers of AB (F), and BC (G), etc., and draw lines from these points through the center of the circle. Draw a circle with any desired radius through these lines, FO, GO, HO, JO, and KO. Draw lines AL, BL, BM, CM, CN, and so on and you will have drawn your 5-pointed star. Shaded effects can be drawn as in section AOG.

How to draw repeated irregular images on a curved line

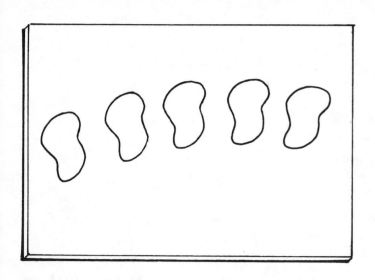

Suppose that you want to draw a design similar to the one at left.

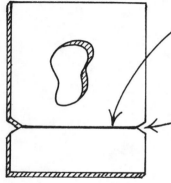

ALIGNING LINE

You could also cut little nicks at the sides to help align.

First cut a template of your image out of cardboard and refine the edges with a gentle rubbing of fine sandpaper. Draw an aligning line under the image.

On your art draw a curved line in pencil as you want it (AB). Your template will align with this line to give you the curve you want for your repeated images. You can build up the template around the edges, gluing little strips of blotting paper or thick cardboard so that your pen will not accidentally smear as you draw the images. Other material (celluloid) can be used to make the template.

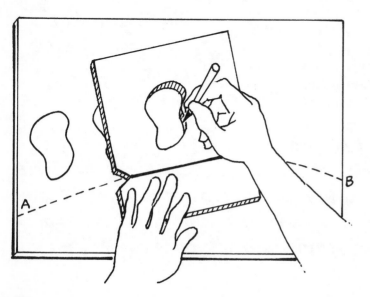

How to draw repeated curved lines in a design

Suppose that you have to draw a curved, or irregular, repeating line as in the example to the left.

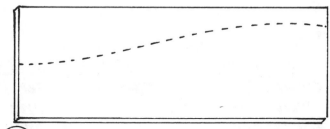

① First design the line on a piece of stiff card or illustration board.

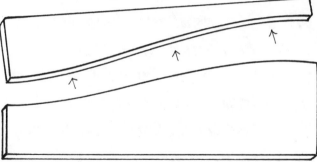

② Then cut this line with a sharp mat knife or stencil knife.

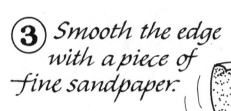

③ Smooth the edge with a piece of fine sandpaper.

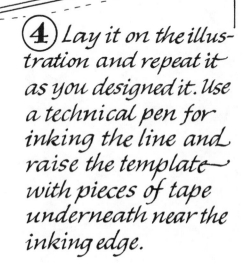

④ Lay it on the illustration and repeat it as you designed it. Use a technical pen for inking the line and raise the template with pieces of tape underneath near the inking edge.

How _any_ regular curve can be made with arcs of circles

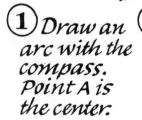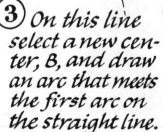

① Draw an arc with the compass. Point A is the center.

② Through this arc draw a straight line.

③ On this line select a new center, B, and draw an arc that meets the first arc on the straight line.

④ Through B draw a straight line, select a new center (C), and draw an arc that meets the last one exactly at one point on the straight line.

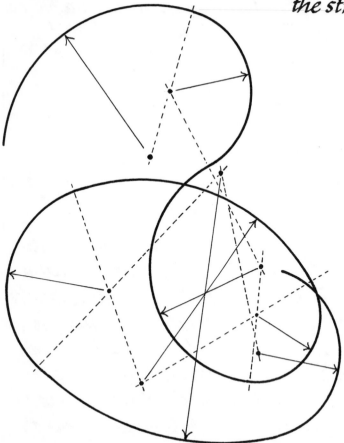

The 4 steps above show the principle by which any regular curved line (one made with arcs of a circle) can be constructed. The essential point is that any 2 consecutive arcs have centers on a common straight line, shown at left with dotted lines ---- the dots are centers of circles used to form the arcs. The consecutive arcs meet at one point only.

The diagram at left is not particularly beautiful. It is drawn for demonstration only.

How to draw a flourished curved line with ellipse templates

In much the same manner as using regular circular arcs to make a curved line ellipse templates can be employed to get a similar curved flourish.

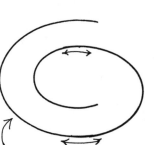

A variation of the diagram to the left.

Spread line can be filled in.

This curve was done with templates. The arrows show the length of overlap common to 2 different sizes.

A spread line can be drawn by moving the template slightly to the left.

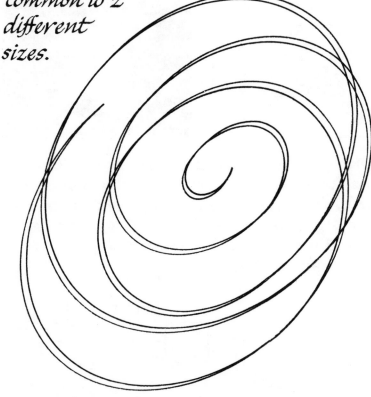

When drawing a curve in this manner, it is good to use only half ellipses. Elliptical joins can be retouched with white paint if necessary.

The flourish to the left is not necessarily beautiful. It was drawn for demonstration purposes only. All arcs and swells were done with templates. Note that these curves do not have the fullness of the flourishes made with arcs of circles.

Optical illusions

Illusions in art are fascinating, and most people enjoy them. A few are shown here.

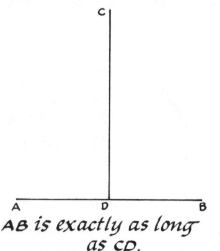

AB is exactly as long as CD.

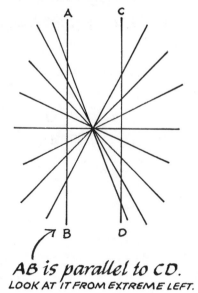

AB is parallel to CD.
LOOK AT IT FROM EXTREME LEFT.

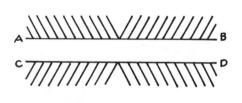

Line AB is parallel to CD.

Do you "read" the circles from top to bottom or bottom to top?

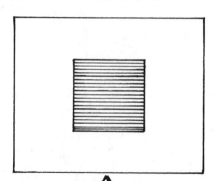

A

B

The gray area in B appears to be lighter than the gray area in A. If the white in A were orange and the gray in A were green, the enclosed square would appear to be blue. If the black in B were blue and the gray in B were green, the square area would appear yellow-green.

AB appears to be shorter than BC. They are both the same size.

All boxes to the right are same size.

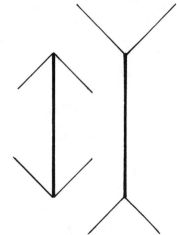

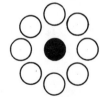

The lopsided figure in the center is a perfect circle.

The line at left appears to be smaller than the line to the right. They are both the same length.

The center circle at top appears to be larger than the bottom solid circle. They are both the same.

The white area to left appears to be much whiter than the white area to the right.

The line AB seems to curve. It is perfectly straight.

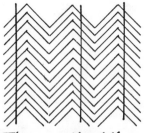

The vertical lines are perfectly parallel.

NOTE

A technique invented in ancient Greece that was popular in France was to paint flat walls with flutes and columns, and very ornate illusions of objects. This style is called "trompe l'oeil."

How to enlarge images by the squares method

If you have a photo, layout, or drawing that you want to enlarge and no other convenient method of enlarging is available, such as a photostat machine, the method below is one way to obtain a reasonable enlargement.

TISSUE PAPER

① Attach tissue paper to the image and trace it carefully. Divide the area into any number of squares.

PHOTO OR DRAWING

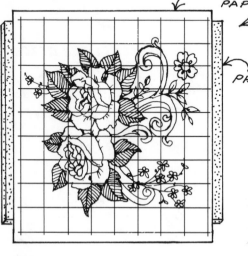

②

On a larger piece of tissue paper or board repeat the number of squares on the smaller sketch. These squares will be much larger. Carefully draw in corresponding squares exactly what is in the small sketch.

You can number the

squares if you wish. The finish may not be an exact enlargement — that depends on how carefully you duplicate the squares.

How to draw reverse, or flopped, images

Suppose you have a drawing such as a girl's profile. Instead of facing in one direction you would like it to face the opposite way. Below are a few simple solutions to your problem.

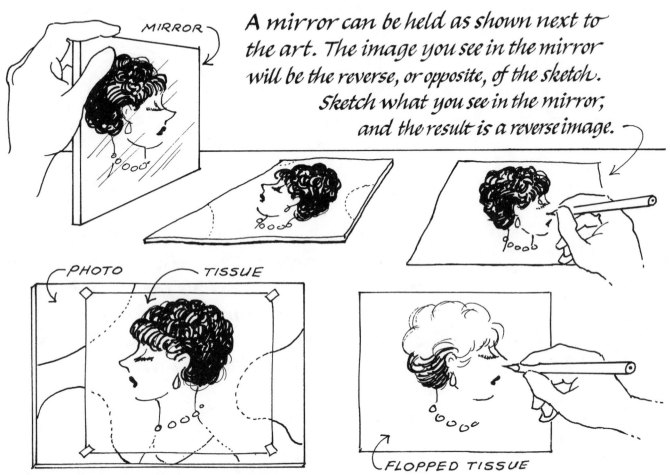

A mirror can be held as shown next to the art. The image you see in the mirror will be the reverse, or opposite, of the sketch. Sketch what you see in the mirror, and the result is a reverse image.

Another method is to trace the art – e.g., a photo – on tissue paper with a good black line (ink, felt nib, soft-pointed pencil). Turn the tissue paper over and redraw (to strengthen) the lines. You can then photostat it larger or smaller. Clear acetate is a great surface for this method.

NOTE.

You can always send your drawing or photo to a commercial photostater and order a "flopped print."

Tips on the care and use of drawing instruments

Every graphic designer should have his own set of good drawing (or drafting) instruments. He should use them properly and take care of them so they will last a long time.

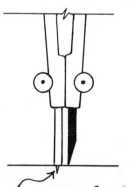

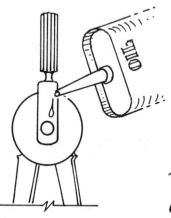

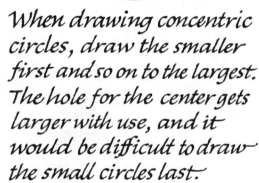

The points of ink or pencil compasses should be slightly longer than the marking point.

Never oil the joints of moving parts on any instrument. They will become too loose and you will be unable to hold your radius.

When drawing concentric circles, draw the smaller first and so on to the largest. The hole for the center gets larger with use, and it would be difficult to draw the small circles last.

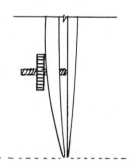

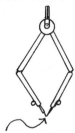

The two blades of the inking point of a compass should meet perfectly—never force the blades beyond the meeting point.

Pencil points should be sharpened to a long, tapering point. Use a sandpaper sharpening block.

The points of jack-knife compasses should meet at one point only for perfect alignment.

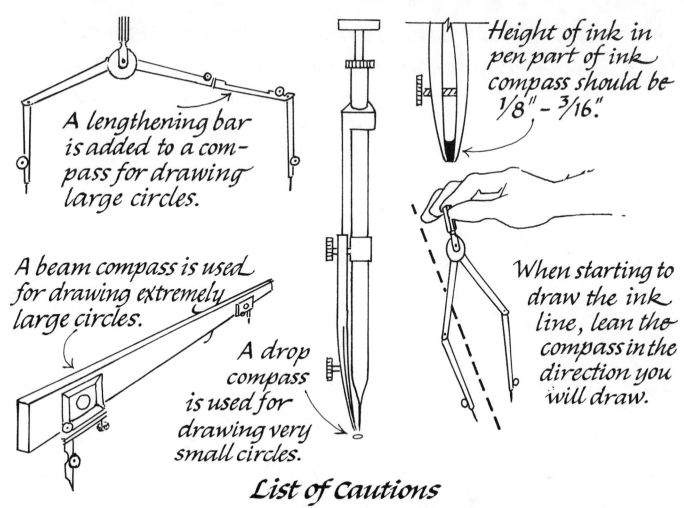

A lengthening bar is added to a compass for drawing large circles.

Height of ink in pen part of ink compass should be 1/8" - 3/16".

A beam compass is used for drawing extremely large circles.

A drop compass is used for drawing very small circles.

When starting to draw the ink line, lean the compass in the direction you will draw.

List of Cautions

① *Never put either end of a wood-clinched pencil in your mouth (It is extremely unsanitary.)*

② *Never jab dividers into the drawing board.*

③ *Never use the same thumb-tack holes to remount a drawing. Small pieces of paper tape are better for holding drawings down on the board.*

④ *Never scrub a drawing all over with an eraser after finishing. It takes the life out of inked lines.*

⑤ *Never begin work before wiping off table and instruments with a small brush.*

⑥ *Never put bow instruments away before cleaning and relaxing the spring.*

Why you should never prepare tools over artwork

When you sharpen pencil points or fill pens with ink, don't do it over your drawing board, especially if the board has artwork on it. You may accidentally mess up the art with droppings.

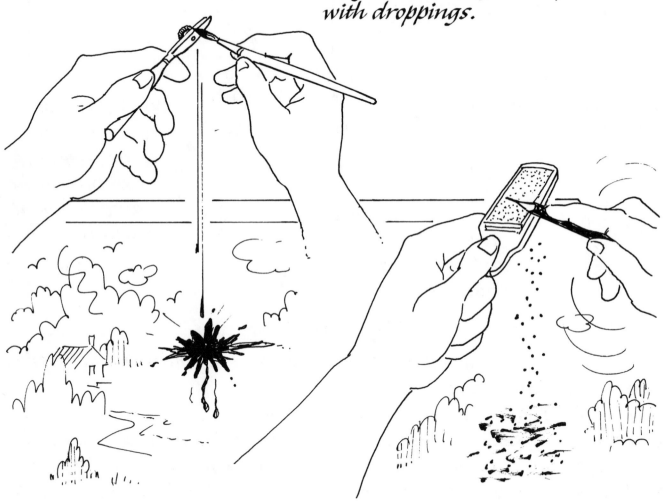

Always do this kind of activity away from your drawing board. A good place is over a trash basket.

How to mark expensive drawing tools

When you buy your own expensive tools (drawing instruments, special pens, mechanical pencils, etc.), you should mark them with your name, initials, or some identifying mark (#). If you work in a large studio, your coworkers will borrow and they may forget to return them, just as you might do. To prevent confusion and possible violent arguments, mark your tools as shown below.

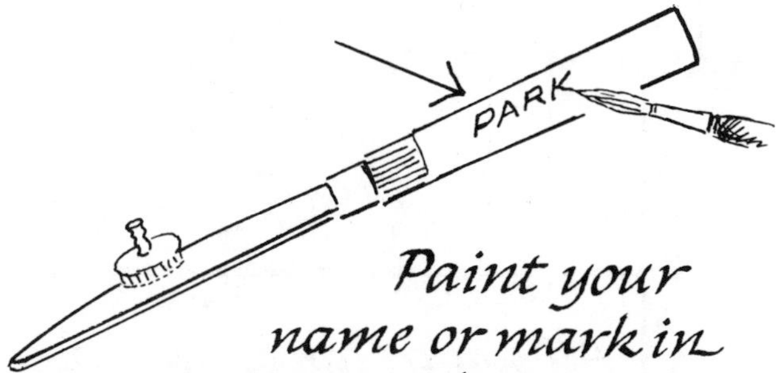

PARK

Paint your name or mark in contrasty color (to background) and then.............. spray your mark with a few layers of varnish spray. Make a mask to protect the other parts

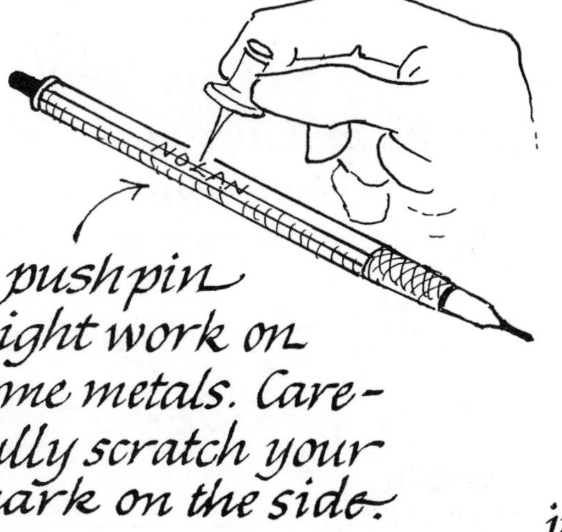

VARNISH FIX

A push pin might work on some metals. Carefully scratch your mark on the side.

You might dip your item in paint, or paint an identifying mark – circle or band of color – around it.

GOLD PAINT

How to use a metal T-square

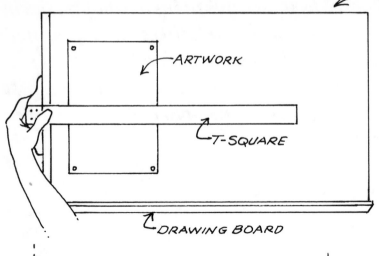

ARTWORK

T-SQUARE

DRAWING BOARD

Always keep work to the left of your drawing board near the head of your T-square. Hold the head of the T-square with your left hand (if you are right-handed). It can be moved easily in this manner.

A T-square can be cleaned regularly by rubbing it with a rag and rubber-cement thinner.

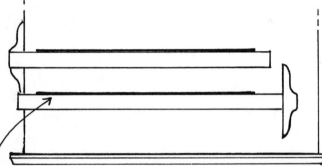

To check a T-square, draw a straight line, turn it upside down, and check the top to see that you draw the exact same line with the same edge.

Never go back and forth — left to right and then right to left — when drawing any line.

Never use the bottom edge of a T-square to draw straight lines, especially ink lines.

Never use T-square as a hammer.

How to store good brushes for a long period of time

You may take a long vacation or break your drawing arm (heaven forbid) and not use your good sable or other brushes as a result. Your brushes should be stored in this case with moth flakes or mothballs in one of the ways suggested below.

A clean old cigar box can hold most of the short brushes. Seal the lid with tape when closed.

All the containers should have either the moth flakes or mothballs generously distributed therein.
Use cardboard rollers from dispenser paper-towel rolls, etc. — a little wax paper for ends.
Mailing tubes are strong and have their own tops.

Take an extra plastic bag at the produce counter of the market. They are great for storing brushes of any size.

How to wash brushes used for acrylic painting

Brushes used in painting with acrylic resin paints can be easily cleaned with alcohol and soap and water.

① Dip brush in alcohol after removing all excess paint on a rag.

② Dip and swish around in mild soap and water

③ Dip for a few minutes into white vinegar.

④ Wash thoroughly in water.

⑤ Shape with fingers when wet-dry and store away for next job.

How to sharpen pencil _points_

The suggestions below are for pencil points on either wood-clinched or mechanical pencils.

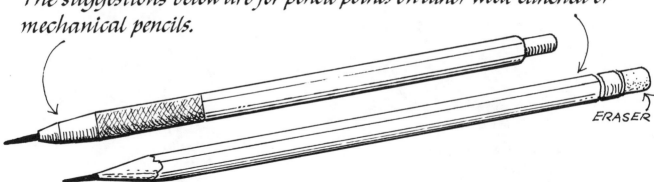

ERASER

There are 2 kinds of points that can be fashioned on a sandpaper or other pencil pointer —

CONICAL   OR   CHISEL

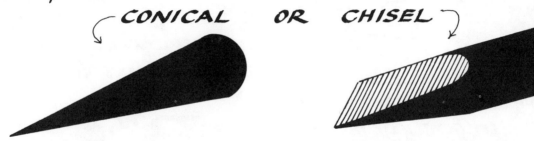

When drawing long lines with a conical point, keep rotating the pencil as you use it. The conical point is also used for lettering.

The flat or chisel edge is preferred by most designers for drawing long straight lines.

Suggestions

1. Keep your pencils sharp. The same is true for mechanical pencils. It's the point that counts.
2. Wipe the lead point after preparing it.
3. The proper grade of softness or hardness is important. You must inspect your writing surface to determine the grade to use.
4. Emery boards and nail files can also be used as pencil pointers.

Inks

Tips on using inks

STICK INK

WET STRING

You can make your own ink.*Sticks of ink and a heavy slate dish can be used with water. After gently grinding, the longer the darker, the ink is filtered with a wet string. This thin ink is great for writing calligraphy or drawing fine line art.

* STICKS ARE AVAILABLE IN ART STORES.

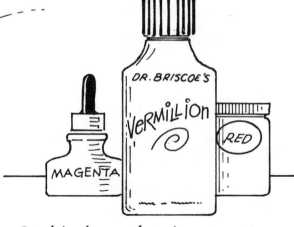

DR. BRISCOE'S VERMILLION

MAGENTA

RED

Red ink or dye is sometimes much thinner than black, allowing you to use it on a fine line drawing. It reproduces just like black.

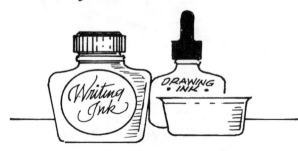

Writing Ink

DRAWING INK

ALCOHOL

RAG

VELLUM

Vellum can be washed with a little alcohol and ink adheres to it much easier.

As a rule you should not mix together 2 different kinds of ink, such as writing ink and waterproof drawing ink. In writing calligraphy that will be erased later a few drops of waterproof ink mixed with writing ink is sometimes good. Throw away excess when finished.

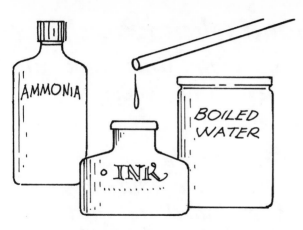

Thin ink with distilled or boiled water, ammonia, or alcohol. Since waterproof ink has shellac in it, alcohol will thin it. Do not use faucet water — it will smell in a short time after capping.

Wash hands frequently when working with ink, especially in writing calligraphy. Greasy hands leave grease spots on paper and pen will skip and blur.

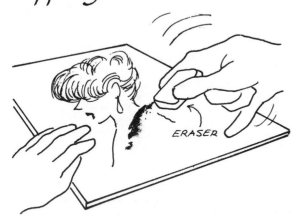

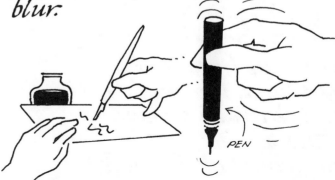

<u>ALWAYS</u> test ink (pen) on scratch paper before using. Jiggle and wipe technical pens until they work.

Be <u>absolutely sure</u> that ink is <u>dry</u> before erasing. Seems trite, but the above happens too frequently in art studios.

Always put top back on ink immediately after using — it will prevent drying out and if knocked over will not make a mess.

87

How to steady your drawing hand when retouching

An aid to your drawing hand in sketching in fine lines in ink or in retouching lettering, etc. is your other hand, as shown below.

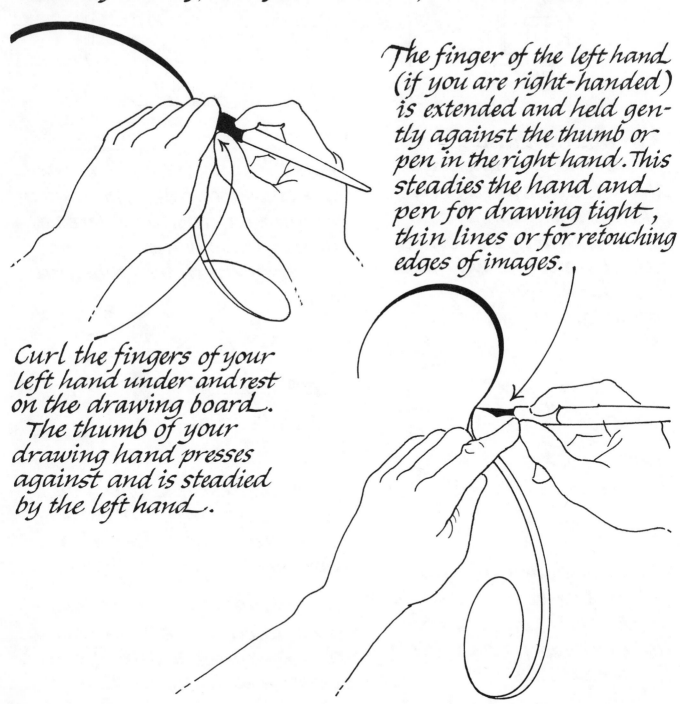

The finger of the left hand (if you are right-handed) is extended and held gently against the thumb or pen in the right hand. This steadies the hand and pen for drawing tight, thin lines or for retouching edges of images.

Curl the fingers of your left hand under and rest on the drawing board. The thumb of your drawing hand presses against and is steadied by the left hand.

Why a blotter should not be used on wet inked lines in art

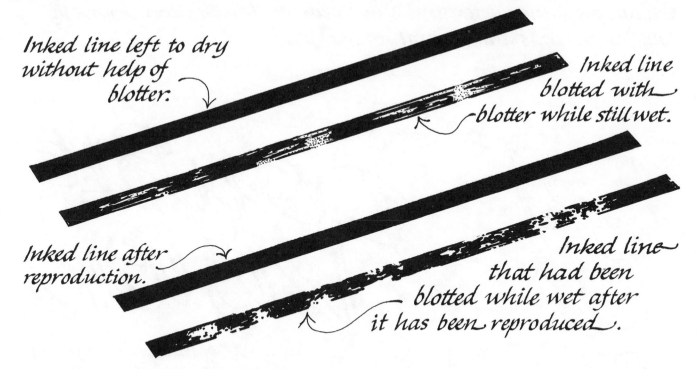

Inked line left to dry without help of blotter.

Inked line blotted with blotter while still wet.

Inked line after reproduction.

Inked line that had been blotted while wet after it has been reproduced.

The demonstration above shows one reason why you should never blot ink lines that will be used for reproduction. If pencil lines have been used to sketch out your drawing first, then inked, dried with a blotter, and erased, the gray of the blotted line will become even weaker. So let your ink lines dry on their own and you will have much happier results in your line-art reproductions. This is particularly true of artwork that uses mainly thin lines, as in crosshatching.

So don't use a blotter. You might also get fuzzy lines or edges that are not sharp and clean.

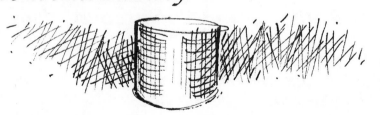

How to get unusual effects with felt-nib pens

You can get unusual textural and linear effects with felt-nib pens by splitting the ends and separating the splits.

STENCIL KNIFE

MARKER OR WIDE FELT-NIB PEN

PENCIL FELT NIB PEN

DOUBLE VISION

All kinds of interesting lettering effects are possible.

Grasses, trees, etc., can be drawn with interesting treatment and thin ink lines added.

All kinds of textural effects are possible. Using different colors of felt-nib pens together gives still more possibilities.

Rubber Cement

Mark "close" and "open" on rubber-cement dispenser

If you have a rubber-cement dispenser with a valve at the end of the spout, you can develop an easy way of opening and closing it as you use it. Simply pick it up at the valve end and twist it open to use. When finished, grasp it again at the valve and twist closed when returning it to your tabouret.

A simple twist of the thumb and forefinger will do the trick.

Attach a piece of paper tape to the side. Mark it "close" and "open" with arrows.

← CLOSE
OPEN →

How to get longer life from a rubber cement pickup

While a rubber-cement pickup is a relatively inexpensive item, you can prolong its life and save some $ in the long run by trimming the collected rubber cement from the pickup with a pair of scissors.

After cleaning in this manner the pickup is almost as good as new and can last for years...

...and you save money, too.

Containers
How to hold and remove tops from bottles and jars

In attempting to remove tops from ink bottles and jars of paint, etc., do not suspend the bottles in the air. Hold them _firmly_ _on_ _a_ _solid_ _table top_ and then remove the top by twisting back and forth. _Never_ open jars or bottles over artwork or illustration board.

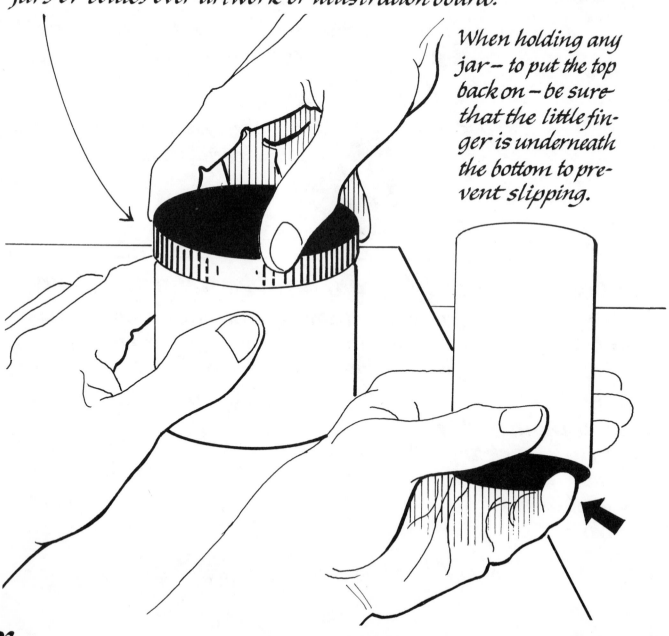

When holding any jar – to put the top back on – be sure that the little finger is underneath the bottom to prevent slipping.

How to prevent watercolor caps from sticking

One of the most annoying things that can happen to a designer or water-color artist is to pick up a tube of paint that he or she has used before and not to be able to get the cap off. He tries a match, hot water, and twisting back and forth with pliers, but it will not come off. Here are 2 suggestions that may help you in this situation.

Replace the plastic caps with metal ones. When discarding old tubes, save all the metal caps – they will be less likely to stick to the top of the tube.

A little lubricating jelly painted on the threads of the tube and cap will help keep caps from freezing shut again.

You can buy in a drug store for a modest price a small tube of lubricating jelly. It is water-soluble and extremely slow in drying.

Glycerine (drug store) can also be used. It, too, is water-soluble and slow-drying. It is sometimes used to help keep colors from drying too fast.

How to prevent mold from forming in jars of watercolor

Mold forms in jars of paint that haven't been opened for awhile because of bacterial activity. There are a few hints below on what you can do to minimize this action.

Instead of using regular faucet water (with bacteria) for thinning color, boil some water (killing bacteria) and keep this boiled water in a small container in the studio for thinning colors in jars.

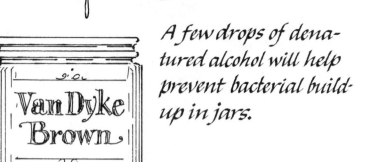

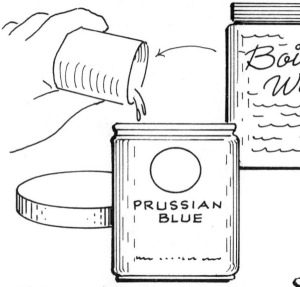

Blues and browns are especially prone to bacterial action.

Of course, jars should be tightly sealed when not in use. Bacteria in the air may get in if they are not tight.

A few drops of denatured alcohol will help prevent bacterial build-up in jars.

How to remove plies from the back of illustration board

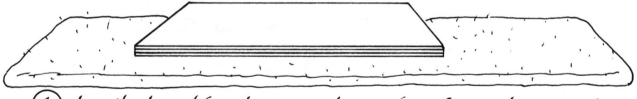

① Lay the board face down on a clean, soft surface, such as a towel.

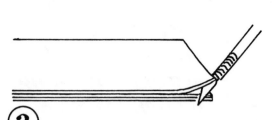

② Separate a ply at a corner with a stencil knife.

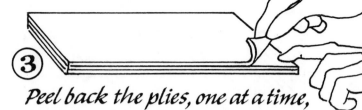

③ Peel back the plies, one at a time, holding the rest of the board with your other hand.

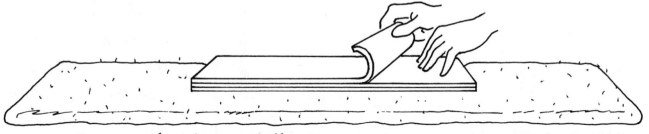

④ Remove the ply carefully. Remove all loose pieces with the knife held almost parallel to the board.

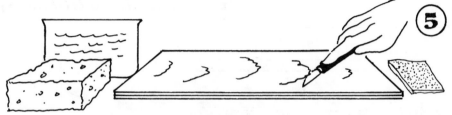

⑤ In removing ply it may help to dampen the back with a sponge and water.

When dry, the entire back surface can be gently smoothed by rubbing it with sandpaper.

How to compensate for thick boards

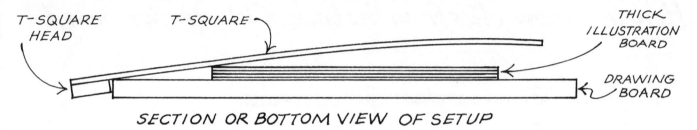

T-SQUARE HEAD

T-SQUARE

THICK ILLUSTRATION BOARD

DRAWING BOARD

SECTION OR BOTTOM VIEW OF SETUP

Sometimes it is awkward to manipulate your T-square when working on thick items on your drawing board. To compensate for this thickness, simply cut a strip of heavy board (illustration board) and attach it to the extreme left of your board. The T-square will then ride on this strip making your work much easier. Be sure that the head of the T-square can still "grab" the left side of the drawing board.

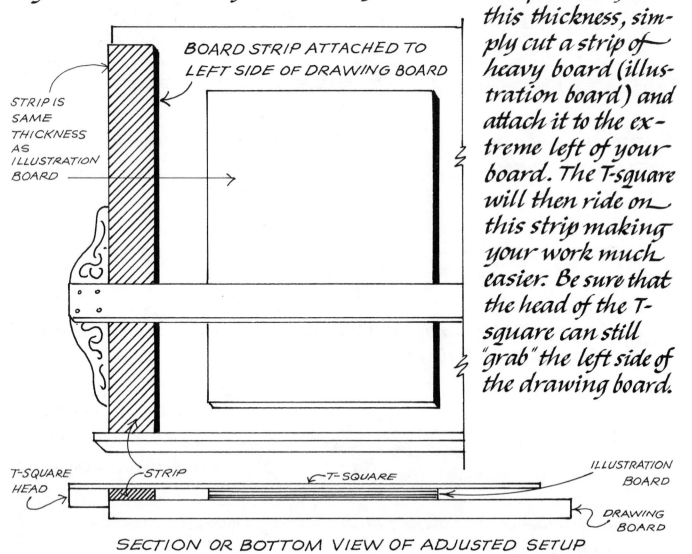

BOARD STRIP ATTACHED TO LEFT SIDE OF DRAWING BOARD

STRIP IS SAME THICKNESS AS ILLUSTRATION BOARD

T-SQUARE HEAD

STRIP

T-SQUARE

ILLUSTRATION BOARD

DRAWING BOARD

SECTION OR BOTTOM VIEW OF ADJUSTED SETUP

How to save watercolor paper

If you are using good, expensive watercolor paper and paint a bad painting or have an accident that ruins the painting, don't throw the paper away. It can be "saved" for another painting. Soak the entire painting in a bathtub or sink full of warm, clean water. You can agitate the painting by gently rubbing with a soft rag or brush. Try not to disturb the fibers of the paper.

When finished washing, hang the paper to dry and then stretch it for a new painting. Blotting it with large blotters may aid in drying.

The surface can again be agitated from time to time with a soft rag and bristle brush. Papers cleaned in this manner can be used more than twice.

A regular garden hose can be used to gently spray the color from the paper.

How to prevent paper cuts while handling sheets of paper or thin cards

Thin white cotton gloves can be worn to minimize paper cuts when handling large amounts of paper or thin cards. If you are working on a large, thin illustration board and must move it around a lot, you can also wear the gloves. If you do not want to remove them, cut off the fingers of the glove so that you have complete freedom in using art tools.

They can be worn while filing large amounts of cards or papers. If you have ever had a nasty paper cut, you will wear gloves the next time.

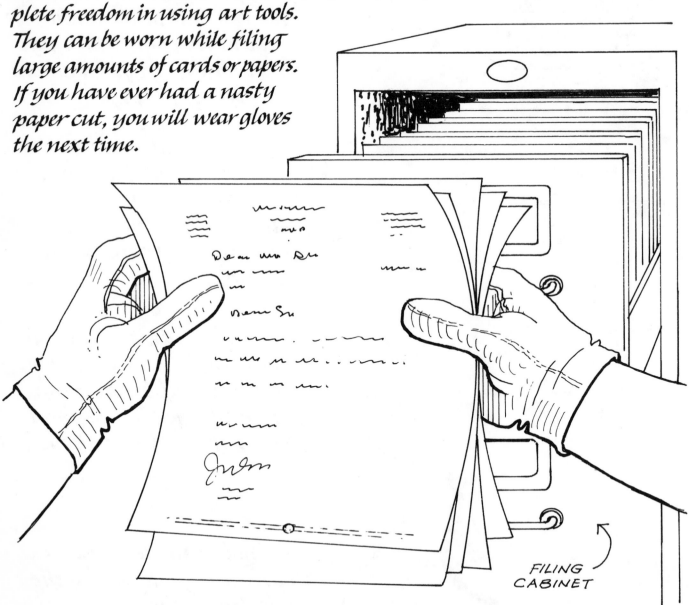

FILING CABINET

How to reinforce holes for pages of your notebook

If you have looseleaf notebooks for keeping all sorts of information (new tools, new typefaces, etc.), the holes in the sheets may become torn in time. To avoid this, follow the instructions below to reinforce the pages.

Adhere pieces of white tape to both sides of the paper where the holes will appear.

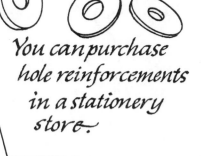

You can purchase hole reinforcements in a stationery store.

Most studios have a 3-hole puncher, which will

save time in punching holes. You hold the sheet in place and lower the top to punch all 3 holes at once.

Mark and punch holes with a hole puncher. Pages can then be put into notebook.

NOTE PAPER SHEET

Tape
Tape tips

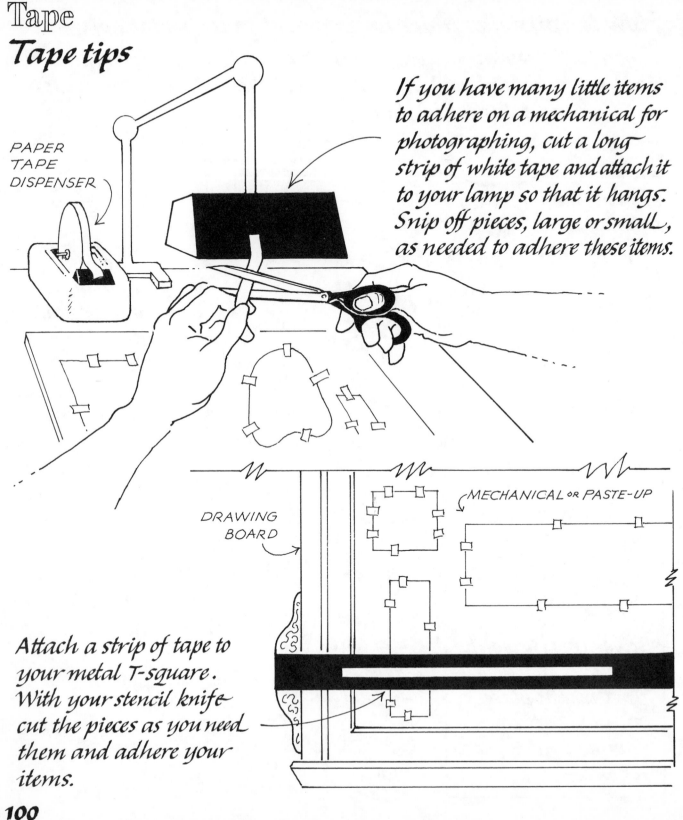

PAPER
TAPE
DISPENSER

If you have many little items to adhere on a mechanical for photographing, cut a long strip of white tape and attach it to your lamp so that it hangs. Snip off pieces, large or small, as needed to adhere these items.

DRAWING
BOARD

MECHANICAL OR PASTE-UP

Attach a strip of tape to your metal T-square. With your stencil knife cut the pieces as you need them and adhere your items.

How to make dried-up masking tape like new again

If you have an old roll of paper or masking tape that has dried and stuck together, follow the instructions below to make it almost like new again.

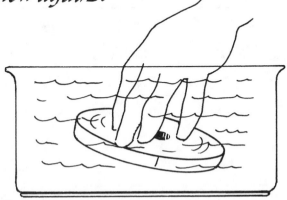

① Soak the roll in water for about 10 seconds.

② Then heat it in the oven until it is warmed through. Set the oven at 250°. It should take a few minutes. Peel off some tape as a test. If it is beyond saving — heave it in file 13.

How to find ends of tapes on rolls easily

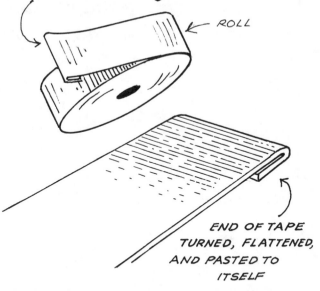

ROLL

END OF TAPE TURNED, FLATTENED, AND PASTED TO ITSELF

It is very annoying to pick up a roll of tape and pick around with your fingernails to try to find the end. By simply turning the end back on itself about ¼" when you have finished using it you will have no trouble finding the end next time.

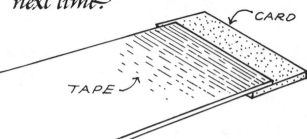

CARD

TAPE

Another simple method is to adhere a small piece of card to the end of the tape.

Frames

How to repair old picture frames

An old picture frame can be cleaned and refinished with a few repair ideas, shown below, perhaps saving you the cost of a new one.

Small scratches on gold frames can be rubbed with a matching gold wax-based paste using a small folded cloth.

First dry-clean the frame with gentle strokes of a small bristle brush. Then dip cotton into denatured alcohol and gently rub the frame to remove caked-on dirt. Do not rub hard. If the frame is covered with gold leaf or gold paint, apply ammonia and water with a soft brush and blot dry. Do not rub.

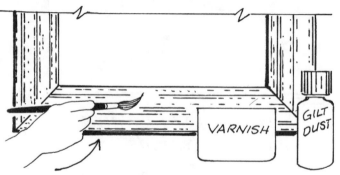

Clean the scratch marks, apply varnish, and, when tacky-dry, pat on gilt powder. When dry the next day, lightly buff the area with clean cotton.

In cleaning a palette knife, toothpick, or smooth sandpaper can help the job, but do not overdo the rubbing. Steel wool and your finger are other "tools."

Scratches on other finished frames besides gold can be touched up with sticks or stains that match. Ornate frames can be built up with gesso, vinyl, or acrylic speckling paste, which you can buy in paint or hardware stores.

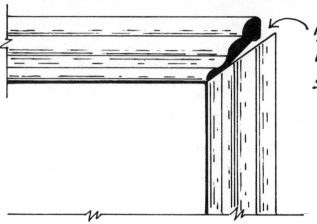

If frame is warped and corners become separated, clean the joints, sandpaper, and glue together.

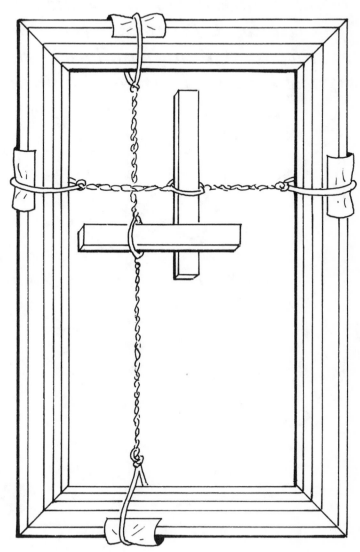

Wrap strong twine around frame (near joints) as shown here.

"Tourneguet" with small pieces of wood but do not pull, or bow, the sides of the frame. Protect the frame edges with folded cards.

On simple fractures clean as best you can and apply glue and tourneguets, patching with plastic wood if necessary. When dry rub with fine sandpaper. Then apply finish and buff with a soft rag.

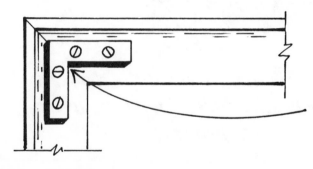

Flat angle irons can be screwed into the back corners if the frame has flat sides on the back. Angle in the screws to pull the pieces of frame together.

Photocopiers
How to position art in your own photostat machine

If you have a photostat machine in your studio and have been wasting prints because you are not positioning your art on the copyboard correctly in relation to the negative before printing keep 2 large L-shaped pieces of black cards handy and use as shown below. You should have no trouble henceforth by wasting prints — and money.

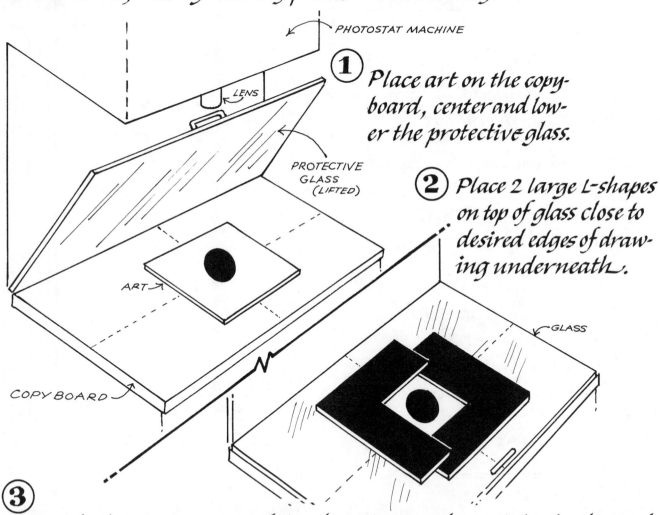

PHOTOSTAT MACHINE

LENS

PROTECTIVE GLASS (LIFTED)

ART

COPYBOARD

GLASS

① *Place art on the copyboard, center and lower the protective glass.*

② *Place 2 large L-shapes on top of glass close to desired edges of drawing underneath.*

③ *Inside the viewing part of the photostat machine sight the desired area, which is easier to see because of the black edges. Position your negative accordingly and shoot. No more wasted prints !!*

How to get good copier prints of tracing paper designs

Most of the models of copying or duplicating machines have buttons to push if you want darker prints. If you use tracing paper (or other transluscent-paper) drawings or designs, you must back up with white card or heavy opaque paper to get a good print – even though the button on the machine is pushed for more contrast. Black ink drawings on frosted acetate are handled in the same way.

TAPE

DESIGN

WHITE MOUNT CARD

Attach the design close to the edges of the card or paper so that it will fit in the machine.

A shiny, glossy white card is great for mounting - it reflects more light.

Don't forget to push the right button.

DARKER   LIGHTER

← COPYING MACHINE →

How to use the copier for a variety of color roughs

If you or the boss likes the sketch you just made but doesn't know what colors to use, make copies of your sketch on the copier and you can make as many different color sketches as you wish. The client will have a better chance to select the "right" one.

It does't matter if your art is line or tone – the images will reproduce. If not, there are adjustments on the copier to make them lighter or darker.

How to make an expedient proportional scale

In an extreme emergency when you have to enlarge something proportionately, the device below may help. It must be noted that, while it is a convenience, it is not precisely accurate.

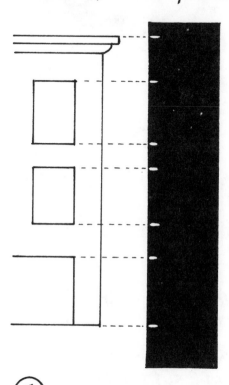

It cannot be emphasized too much that this is not a precise and accurate enlargement BUT it may help if close is good enough.

① On a wide elastic band mark off the elements you want to enlarge.

② Stretch the band to the overall length desired, mark off the points, and redraw the enlargement.

ENLARGEMENT

Secure ends with tape or pushpins.

How to make your own circle cutter

If you have a pencil compass, you can very easily make your own circle cutter. Your art store may have a blade to fit your compass where the lead goes, but if you had one and lost it or if you never had one — make one by following the instructions below.

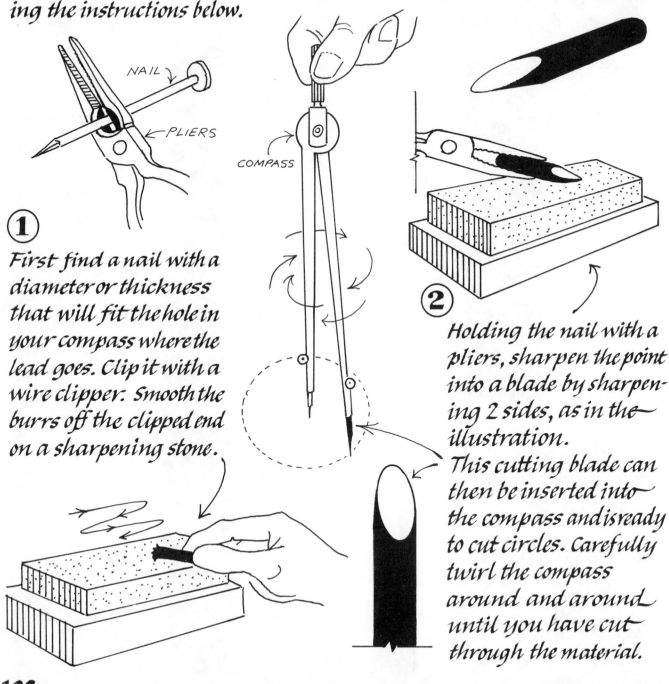

NAIL

PLIERS

COMPASS

①

First find a nail with a diameter or thickness that will fit the hole in your compass where the lead goes. Clip it with a wire clipper. Smooth the burrs off the clipped end on a sharpening stone.

②

Holding the nail with a pliers, sharpen the point into a blade by sharpening 2 sides, as in the illustration.

This cutting blade can then be inserted into the compass and is ready to cut circles. Carefully twirl the compass around and around until you have cut through the material.

How to make your own "ruler"

There may be an occasion when you want to measure something, or establish a proportion and do not have a convenient measuring device handy. It is a simple matter to make your own ruler and obtain the proportions you want.

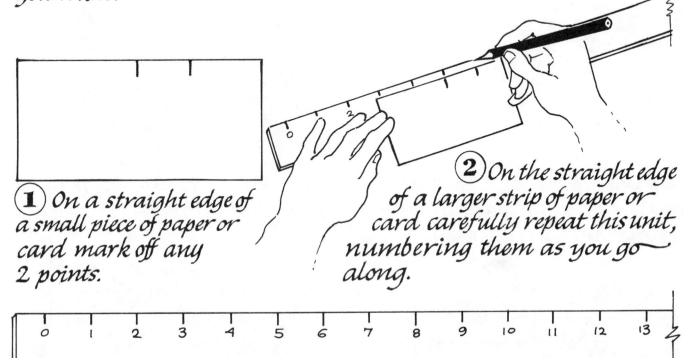

1 On a straight edge of a small piece of paper or card mark off any 2 points.

2 On the straight edge of a larger strip of paper or card carefully repeat this unit, numbering them as you go along.

| 0 | 1 | 2 | 3 | 4 | 5 | 6 | 7 | 8 | 9 | 10 | 11 | 12 | 13 |

3 You have now made your own measuring device which can be used to measure units of relative distances.

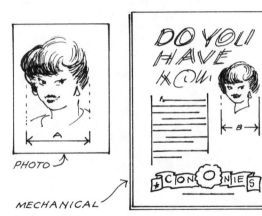

PHOTO

MECHANICAL

In the example to the left you want to reduce the photo to a photostat the width of B on the marks on the mechanical. Suppose that the photo measures 10 units and your mechanical area measures 5 units, using your "ruler." You would now order a photostat for 50% reduction (10:5).

How to make a transfer sheet

Rolls of transfer sheets for any purpose can be bought in art stores but they are a little expensive for modest budgets. Here's how you can make your own – for any purpose.

① *On a piece of tracing paper use the side of a soft pencil and rub the entire surface in one direction.*

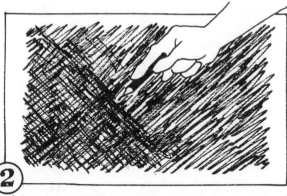

② *Now rub the entire surface in the opposite direction.*

③ *Rub the entire area with your finger or a cotton ball.*

④ *A slightly damp cotton ball with a drop of rubber cement thinner can be rubbed over the area after ③ and, starting at ①, repeat all steps.*

A hard-pointed 5 H or 6 H pencil should be used to transfer the image, with the transfer sheet between. Stabilo pencils (all colors) can be used to make transfer sheets to transfer images onto glass or glossy photos. Colored pastels can also be used instead of graphite pencils.

How to make a good mat

The proportions for the width of the mat – from all sides to the hole for the picture – is a matter of personal choice. Most artists will agree to the points expressed below on making a good mat, even though there are always the exceptions, for various effects. to these "rules." First let's look at bad mats.

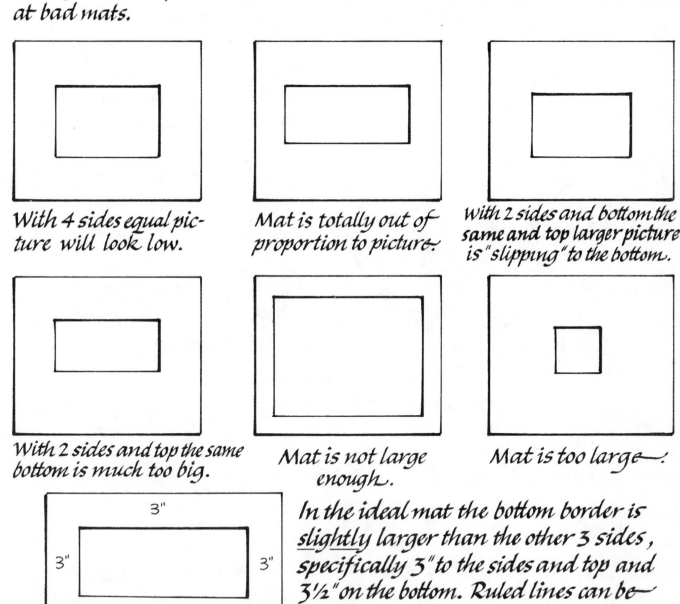

With 4 sides equal picture will look low.

Mat is totally out of proportion to picture.

With 2 sides and bottom the same and top larger picture is "slipping" to the bottom.

With 2 sides and top the same bottom is much too big.

Mat is not large enough.

Mat is too large.

In the ideal mat the bottom border is _slightly_ larger than the other 3 sides, specifically 3" to the sides and top and 3½" on the bottom. Ruled lines can be added.

How to make your own portfolio

Expensive leather portfolios are impressive, but what counts most is what is inside. You can make your own portfolio for a modest sum and it will do the job. Neatness and cleanliness, of course, count, and you should keep this in mind.

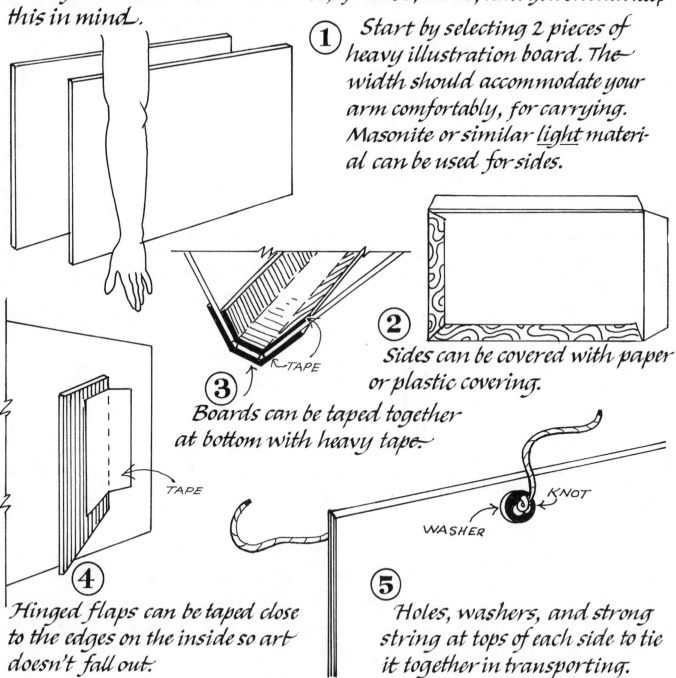

① Start by selecting 2 pieces of heavy illustration board. The width should accommodate your arm comfortably, for carrying. Masonite or similar _light_ material can be used for sides.

② Sides can be covered with paper or plastic covering.

③ Boards can be taped together at bottom with heavy tape.

④ Hinged flaps can be taped close to the edges on the inside so art doesn't fall out.

⑤ Holes, washers, and strong string at tops of each side to tie it together in transporting.

Homemade Holders *and* Containers

How to make a convenient pegboard holder for tools

A small pegboard and frame can be constructed to be positioned to the left of your drawing board, and hooks installed where you want them. It is a handy arrangement to hold tools frequently used in your daily work.

How to make an expedient pen and brush holder and tissue dispenser

There may be an occasion when you want a setup like the one to the right. A roll of toilet tissue can serve as a handy little item when used in this manner, as the tissues have many uses at the drawing board.

How to make two brush holders

Regular plastic soda straws can be cut in half and taped to the edge of your drawing board to hold brushes that you are working with.

Brush can easily be lifted from and inserted into straw.

This is an expedient method of holding brushes. More permanent storage would be in a jar.

Tape could be reinforced with push pins.

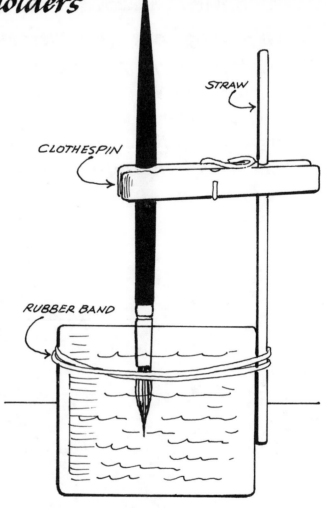

CLOTHESPIN

STRAW

RUBBER BAND

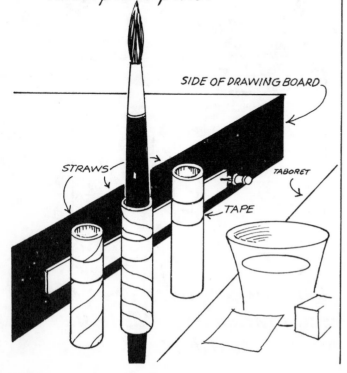

SIDE OF DRAWING BOARD

STRAWS

TABORET

TAPE

Brush can be suspended handily in water and held by a clothespin and drinking straw which are attached to each other. The straw, or a small flat stick, is held to the water glass with a rubber band. Glass should have flat sides.

How to make a holder for delicate pens and knives

Save expensive cigar containers or ask someone who smokes them (cigars) to save the containers for you. Some toothbrushes are bought in similar cases. They come in glass, metal, or plastic. They are handy and safe for carrying stencil knives, technical pens, or other unguarded pens. Be sure that the container is long enough to accommodate the pen or knife. You may have other things you wish to store.

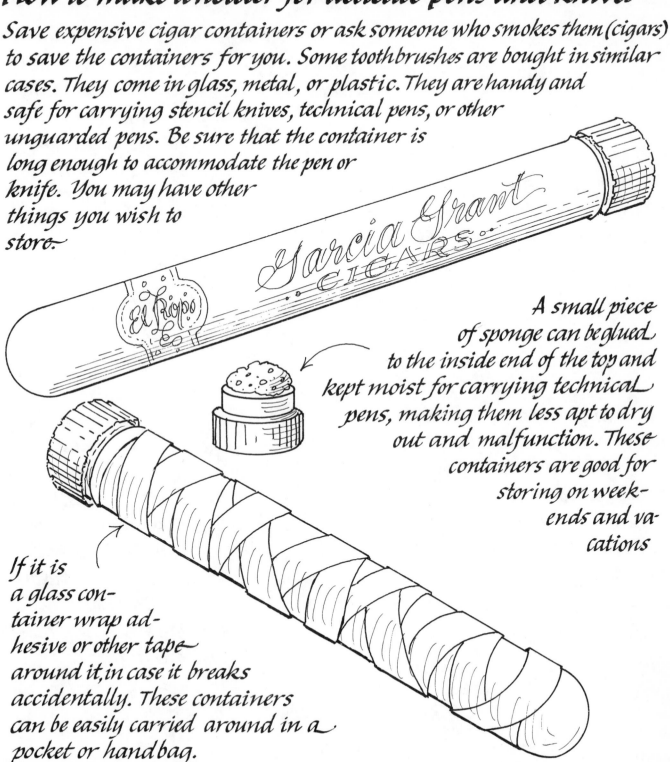

A small piece of sponge can be glued to the inside end of the top and kept moist for carrying technical pens, making them less apt to dry out and malfunction. These containers are good for storing on week-ends and vacations

If it is a glass container wrap adhesive or other tape around it, in case it breaks accidentally. These containers can be easily carried around in a pocket or handbag.

How to make inexpensive water and paint containers

Common household plastic containers can be cut down to make no-cost water and paint containers. They can be as large as you want, depending on the size container you start with.

Cut a large plastic container to make a large water "jar." Measure and mark the cutting edge (indicated by the dotted line above) and cut with the mat knife.

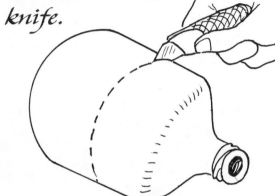

Smaller containers can be cut from small plastic bottles. Pill containers are great for small amounts of mixed colors. A cover of wax paper with a rubber band will keep the color moist overnight.

How household plastic containers can be used as water holders for outdoor watercolors

If you take "field trips" to the country to paint in watercolor and are not near a ready water supply (stream, pond, etc.), you can carry the water with you in one of the household plastic squeeze containers. They come in large and small sizes, can be easily cleaned, and will not leak if the tops are secured.

Ammo Cleaner

DiSHWAter LiQiD

COLD WATER Stuff

Nolan's Bleach

SOAP

One can be cut down for a water container while you work.

SOAP

How to make a paint "hell-box"

The word hell-box came from the printing trades. Used metal in the printer's shop was thrown into a hell box and melted down for reuse in casting new type. You can use old watercolor paint residue in your water jar and chips from your color spread cards to make your own hell box.

Residue from water jars and scrapings from palettes are saved in the hellbox. Gum water (you can buy it in art stores) or gum arabic crystals (art store) can be added to give it body and an adhesive quality. The resulting color will surprise you when used from the hellbox. We dare you to try and match it by mixing your own.

WATER JAR

SPATULA

RESIDUE FROM WATER JAR

HELL BOX

LID TO HELL BOX

GUM WATER

A

GUM ARABIC CRYSTALS

SPATULA

SCRAPINGS OF PAINT FROM PALETTE OR SPREAD CARD

HELL BOX

LID

How to make expensive-looking boards from cheap cards

You can laminate colored papers (coloraid, textured, gift-wrap papers, etc.) onto the backs of cheap cardboards, such as the backs of sketching pads, to get expensive-looking boards.

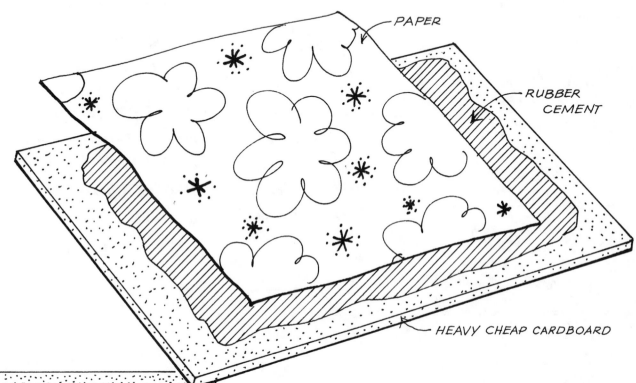

PAPER

RUBBER CEMENT

HEAVY CHEAP CARDBOARD

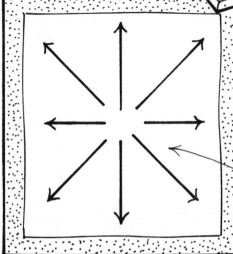

Paper is dry-mounted onto the card. Slip sheets can be used. Pressure with the soft back of your hand is better than a celluloid triangle (or similar hard tool). A protective sheet of paper should cover the paper as you apply pressure from the center out to the edges.
Card can later be trimmed to a smaller size if desired.

How to use small scrap pieces of cards

Leftover pieces of thin cards can be cut into small (2"x 3½") pieces and used in one or more of the ways shown below.

 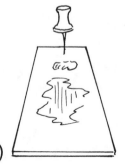 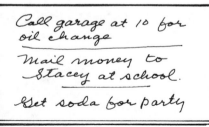

① Scraping together spilled rubber cement and the like.

② Push pin holds card for paint spreader for preparing brush.

③ Use for temporary notes and reminders. Card will fit into wallet with money.

Call garage at 10 for oil change
Mail money to Stacey at school.
Get soda for party

TAPE

Jinnie Call Bill urgent! Patrice

④ Write notes for others (telephone messages, visitors, etc.).

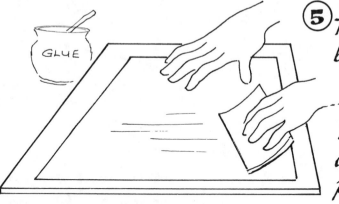

GLUE

⑤ They can be used as brayers for smoothing down large pasted areas.

PLEASE KEEP DOOR CLOSED

WET PAINT

WILL BE BACK AT 2 PM J.M.

⑥ Use for small temporary signs.

How to use tissue and vellum pad backs over again

Instead of discarding the backs of paper pads (tissue, vellum, bond, etc.) save them for possible uses as demonstrated below.

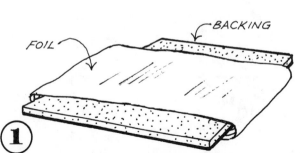

① Stretch aluminum foil around them and use for a disposable paint palette.

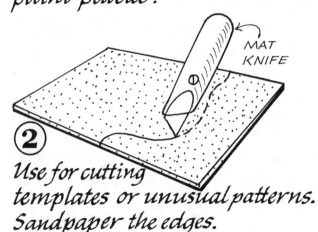

② Use for cutting templates or unusual patterns. Sandpaper the edges.

③ Laminate colored or patterned paper onto them for expensive-looking heavy boards.

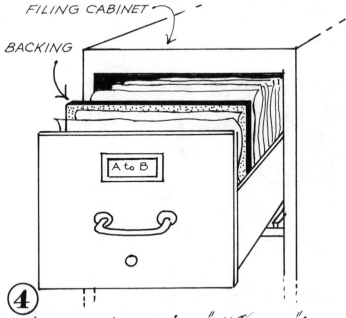

④ They can be used as "stiffeners" in floppy files. Insert them here and there so that papers don't collapse.

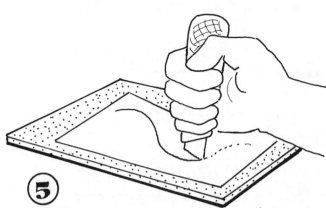

⑤ Use as a cutting-board backing to save your table tops and drawing boards.

Some tips on storing oil paint and cleaning brushes

Preserving leftover oil paints is the concern of everyone who works in oil. Here are some suggestions for "saving" them for short times—saving the artist some money as well.

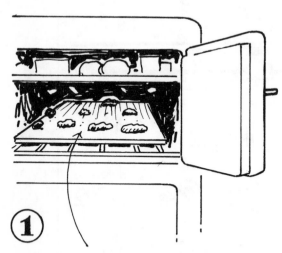

① Store them in the freezer — they will keep indefinitely.

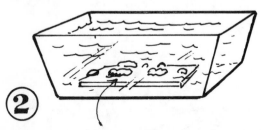

② Use a glass palette and submerge the entire palette in a convenient large pan of water. Good for a week but not much longer — some oxidation with the pigment does take place in the water.

③ Use old plastic pill containers. Seal the lid edges with tape. Old aluminum airtight cans, which hold 35 mm film, can also be used.

④ Oil brushes should be cleaned after each painting session. Rub excess paint onto a rag, wash in turpentine and wash with white soap and warm water many times. Kerosene or mineral spirits may be used.

The addition of a small piece of screen on the bottom of the jar may help rub out some of the paint from the heel of the brush.

How to use art supplies found in the medicine cabinet

Many of the items found in the bathroom medicine cabinet can be used as tools to aid the graphic artist. Examples and their uses are shown below.

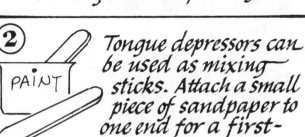

(1) Q-tips and swabs can be used for cleaning in difficult places, bleaching photos, and as a "brush" for certain paint effects.

(2) Tongue depressors can be used as mixing sticks. Attach a small piece of sandpaper to one end for a first-class pencil pointer.

Talcum powder dusts and dries hands on wet or humid days. **(3)** TALC · DUSTING POWDER

(4) AMMO · Ammonia can be used to thin down or clean waterproof ink.

An eyedropper can **(5)** be used to measure liquids and fill pens.

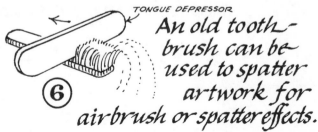

TONGUE DEPRESSOR

(6) An old tooth-brush can be used to spatter artwork for airbrush or spatter effects.

(7) Cotton balls with rubber-cement thinner are great for cleaning purposes and for rubbing charcoal and pastel drawings for effect.

Hydrogen peroxide **(8)** is great for bleaching out areas of a photo. Use Q-tips or swabs to apply it.

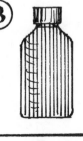

(9) Adhesive tapes can be used to mark bottles and patch busted paint tubes, as can nail polish.

How to make a paper funnel

There may be times when you need a funnel in a hurry. You may be working on a job and need rubber-cement thinner in your dispenser can. You need a funnel and can't find one. If you follow the instructions below, a good temporary funnel can be made in a matter of minutes.

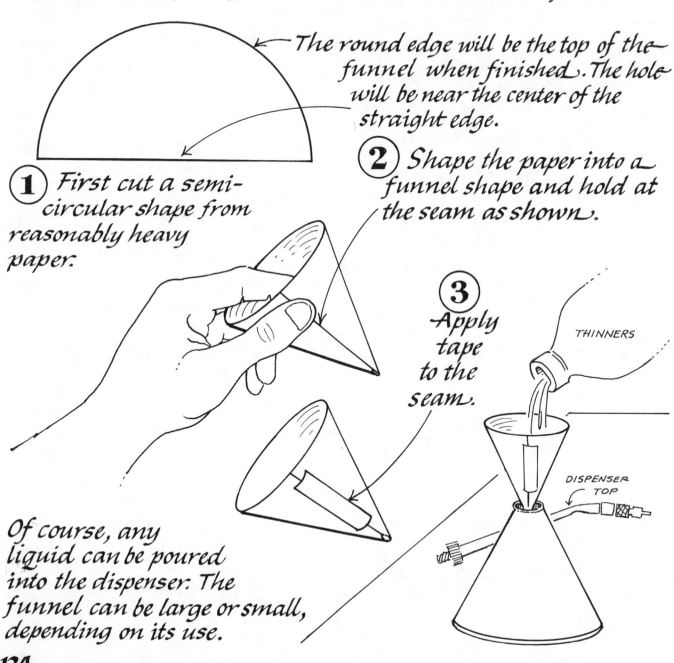

The round edge will be the top of the funnel when finished. The hole will be near the center of the straight edge.

1 First cut a semi-circular shape from reasonably heavy paper.

2 Shape the paper into a funnel shape and hold at the seam as shown.

3 Apply tape to the seam.

THINNERS

DISPENSER TOP

Of course, any liquid can be poured into the dispenser. The funnel can be large or small, depending on its use.

How to make your own sandpaper pencil pointer

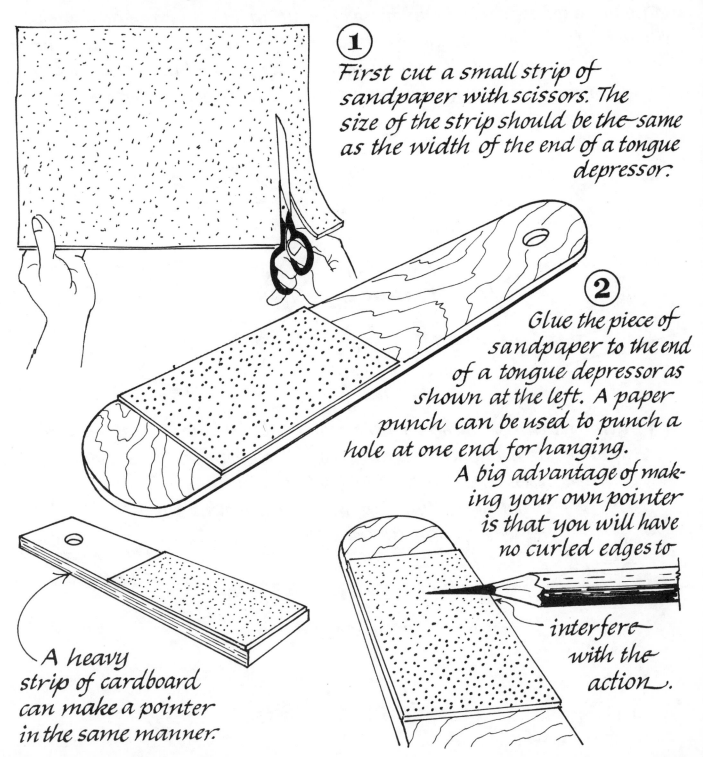

① First cut a small strip of sandpaper with scissors. The size of the strip should be the same as the width of the end of a tongue depressor.

② Glue the piece of sandpaper to the end of a tongue depressor as shown at the left. A paper punch can be used to punch a hole at one end for hanging.

A big advantage of making your own pointer is that you will have no curled edges to interfere with the action.

A heavy strip of cardboard can make a pointer in the same manner.

How to make a "stationary" card palette for mixing paint

When you are preparing your brush by pointing it on a spread card or palette, it is very annoying to have the card move around. On large jobs a large "immovable" palette would be used and you would not have this problem. Here's a suggestion for those small jobs where a small card is used for preparing your paint and brush.

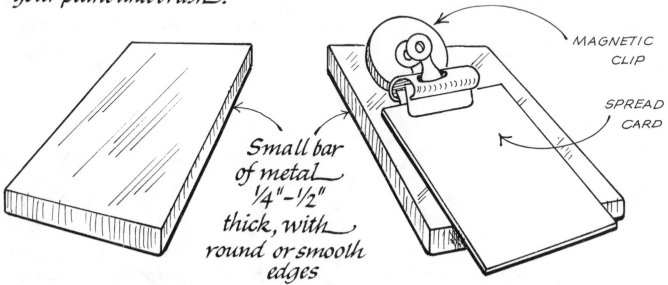

MAGNETIC CLIP

SPREAD CARD

Small bar of metal ¼"–½" thick, with round or smooth edges

A magnetic clip is attached to the upper part of a small, heavy metal bar. The clip holds your spread card, which can easily be replaced when necessary. Your card will not move around the drawing board with this setup. Here are two other simple methods of "holding" your spread card.

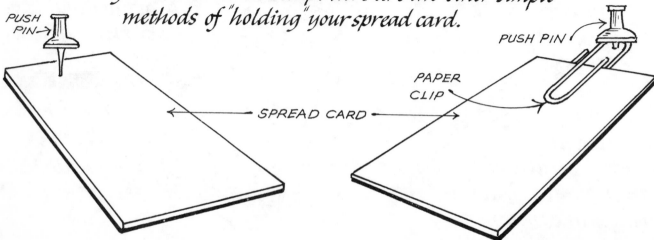

PUSH PIN

PUSH PIN

PAPER CLIP

SPREAD CARD

How to use a burnt cork for shading effects

If charcoal sticks or graphite pieces are not available and you need to achieve a soft shading effect, burned cork might serve your purpose. So save those corks from office parties, etc. The smudged area can be fixed with workable fixative when finished.

Burn the end of the cork carefully after washing the cork well. Apply cork to the desired area and blend or soften with your finger or a piece of cotton.

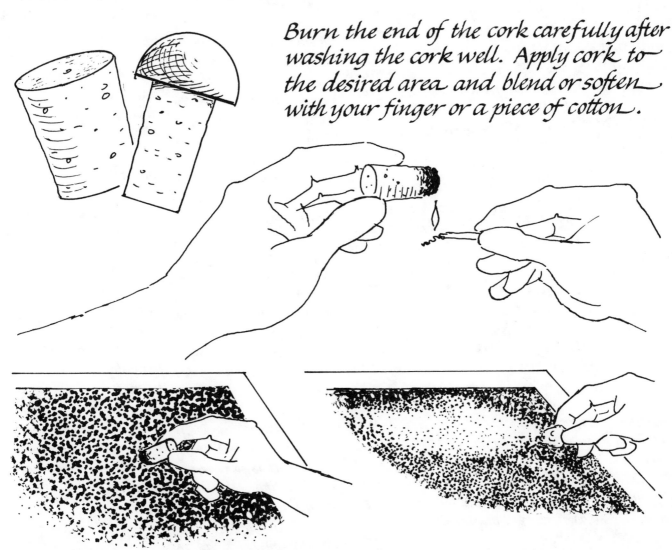

Clouds and rounded shapes on art already done can be reinforced with a soft charcoal tone effect. Kneaded erasers can be used to pick up highlights.

Index